A Soul Returned

A Soul Returned

Kimberly McCrear-Himmons

Copyright © 2024 by Kimberly McCrear-Himmons

All rights reserved. No part of this publication may be reproduced, distributed, or transmitted in any form or by any means, including photocopying, recording, or other electronic or mechanical methods, without the prior written permission of the copyright owner and the publisher, except in the case of brief quotations embodied in critical reviews and certain other noncommercial uses permitted by copyright law. For permission requests, write to the publisher, addressed "Attention: Permissions Coordinator," at the address below.

CITIOFBOOKS, INC.
3736 Eubank NE Suite A1
Albuquerque, NM 87111-3579
www.citiofbooks.com

Hotline: 1 (877) 389-2759
Fax: 1 (505) 930-7244

Ordering Information:
Quantity sales. Special discounts are available on quantity purchases by corporations, associations, and others. For details, contact the publisher at the address above.

Printed in the United States of America.

ISBN-13: Paperback   979-8-89391-322-4
          eBook   979-8-89391-323-1

Library of Congress Control Number: 2024918888

As you eavesdrop into the lives of the women of this story, my prayer is that their existence affects your existence. Although they are fictional characters on paper, please understand that they are each a part of my reality. My prayer is that my reality can help bring a change in your life. Although some of the text is graphic, please know that life offers so many harsh realities that can never be explained or understood. I hope that I cause a leap in your spirit that causes you to speak out to the abuse that has held so many men and women in bondage. My prayer is that any spirit of fear, neglect, or bondage be brought into captivity and bound forever more. I pray that love, compassion, and goodwill be loosed towards all, man and woman. It is time for my story to be told so that others can be heard.

Looking up into the windshield of the car, Kayla could not believe the look that had transpired onto Tyson's face. It was as if he as possessed by the devil himself. His intense gaze bore into her eyes, her mind, and her heart. Kayla felt her heart beating inside of her throat. Fear had literally held her body in one position... on her knees. "Dear God, please tell me that this is not happening!"

"Get up, get up!" a faint voice echoed in her ears. Kayla tried to lift herself up but found her knees planted firmly onto the gravel of the road.

"Girl, you have to get up, now!"

Kayla looked up into Tyson's face and saw the smirk that began to form around his mouth. It was the same look that she had encountered whenever he was ready for battle.

"God, help me," she began to murmur to herself. Kayla suddenly felt a warmth rise up in her spirit. She slowly began to gather her strength so that she could get up. She raised her right leg and planted her foot on the ground. She slowly began to raise her left leg, placed it on the ground, and steadily lifted herself up.

"Baby, now all you have to do is turn around and start running." She listened to her own voice coaching her as if she were a little girl.

She took one last glance at Tyson's face as he watched her. She could not believe that he looked so calm. It was as if nothing was going on. Peace had actually taken up residence within him. In fact, it flowed through him as he slowly pressed on the gas pedal of his car.

This time, Kayla saw the car as it veered in her direction.

"God, God, no! Not again."

No sooner had she finished her silent prayer, the car made contact with her legs again and knocked her to the ground. She did not fall in a quick, jarring way as she had expected. Instead, she fell in slow motion back down to her knees... a position that she had not been in so many years, too many to count.

"Lord, please have mercy on my soul."

Kayla woke up with a start. She could not believe that she was having this nightmare again. It had been a while since she had even seen or heard from Tyson.

Thank goodness that their relationship was over. Kayla could not believe that he had actually hit her with a car. Yet considering how rocky their relationship had been, it wasn't too surprising that it had ended the way that it did.

For six years, Kayla endured the craziness that seemed to surround Tyson wherever he went. In fact, the late night conversations, which eventually turned into arguments and fights, became routine for her. She knew how Tyson's moods could flip at any given moment, and found herself thinking of ways to ease the tension before it ever started. She learned how to get along and how to go along with whatever he said just to keep him happy. Most of the time, it seemed to work. Tyson would get his way and life was all that and a bag of chips. Yet, there were other times when she could not do or say anything right. "Let's get ready to rumble!" All they needed was for Michael Buffer to be in their living room because it was definitely on.

Kayla sat up in her bed and began to think back to those six years when she and Tyson were together. At one point in her life, she tried not to think about that time in her life. It was too traumatic. She did not want to think about the name-calling or the cussing. She did not want to think about the threats and accusations. And she definitely did not want to remember the slaps, punches, and kicks.

How had she ended up in a relationship that was so violent? It went against everything that was in her being, everything that she stood for. She hated fighting, arguing, or any kind of disagreement. She didn't like any form of pain, whatever the package.

Kayla felt tears begin to well up in the corners of her eyes.

"Girl, get yourself together. Don't go there, especially not today." Kayla remembered this day. It was the exact day that she made the one phone call that would save her life. It was the day that she called her family to ask them to come and rescue her from the hell that she had made of her life. It was also the same day the Tyson tried to take her life for the last time when he hit her with the car. Only, that day she decided that she was not going to give it up to him anymore.

Kayla felt a sense of triumph fill her soul. Tyson did not know that when he knocked her to her knees, he did her a favor. In fact, when she tried to get up and was hit again, it was only confirmation for her that she needed to stay on her knees just a little bit longer… To praise God for giving her another lease on life.

Kayla jumped up out of bed and headed off to the bathroom. She turned on the shower and began to take off her nightshirt. She tested the water before she stepped in.

"Ahh," Kayla groaned as the warm pellets of water beat against her body. She felt all the tension that had settled in the pit of her stomach begin to leave. This was exactly what she needed. Water sprayed across her body at just the right angles as the advertisement stated that it should. Kayla remembered the day when she decided to have her bathroom remodeled. She wanted all the extras that would turn her favorite room in the house into her sanctuary and haven.

Kayla couldn't believe that a bathroom could feel so safe. Usually when she thought about a bathroom, she pictured someone coming in, taking care of his or her business, and then leaving out. The smells from soaps, perfume and cologne, curling irons, and its' occupants' bodies had a way of permeating the wallpaper and shower curtains. Although the smallest room in a house, a bathroom played an enormous role in the life of those who inhabited it.

To Kayla, the bathroom became a safety net for her. It was the only room in the house that no one dared to enter without making sure that it was OK. One could never be sure of what they would see or even smell. The bathroom was also the only room in the house that Tyson made sure that there was a lock on the door. Whether it was to read some on his girlie magazines and play with himself in private, or to sip on his forty and smoke a blunt, Tyson made sure that Kayla could not barge in and disturb him.

Kayla had no problems with this because Tyson's den of sin also kept her safe in those times when he decided to harass her. She could lock herself in the bathroom until he fell out into a drunken stupor or even decided to leave the apartment altogether. There she would sit down on the toilet and pray to God to forgive her of all of her sins. There had to be a reason for her to be where she was. Only at that time, Kayla could not or better yet, would not look at the reasons why. That is until this very day.

"Thank you. Thank you. Thank you," Kayla squealed with delight.

Kayla stepped out of the shower and toweled herself off. After lotioning her body, she headed off to her bedroom to get dressed. Today was definitely a very important day. This was the day when all her dreams would come true. Kayla could not believe that everything was finally falling into place.

Today was the day when she would finally open the doors to Soul Simplicities, a safe haven for women who needed to leave out of desperate situations. Starting as a mere thought in her mind, Kayla never believed that she was actually now involved in such a project. God surely has a way of taking our bad situations and turning them around for good.

Kayla remembered the tough time she had of actually leaving Tyson. Fear had become her best friend. She was afraid of him and the life that he offered her. She was also afraid of venturing out into the unknown if she decided to leave him. It was rough because her whole life had revolved around what Tyson wanted and needed. She never took the time to put herself first.

Although she made a decent salary as a teacher, it never seemed that it would be enough to survive on her own. She and Tyson shared everything including their paychecks. Although they were not married, they lived together as man and wife wannabees.

Then, there was the fear of being alone. No matter how tense their relationship became, it also had become a crutch for her because she knew that she wasn't by herself. He was someone who she could lean on, especially in those times when she needed to get motivated. Looking back on those years, she did not realize how much she needed to be pushed to do something. Tyson had a way of doing this. He would sometimes use kind words that made her want to make him proud. Other times, he would give ultimatums that would ultimately cause her to show him that he was not going to dictate what she was going to do. Other times he forced change, whether she liked it or not. In every way, Kayla realized that she had never initiated anything.

That's why it had been so hard for her to get going even after she finally did leave him. Even though he wasn't physically present anymore, she still heard his voice in the background. "Come on, baby, you can do it!" or "Yeah, you think so. I dare you to do that." Or "Wait until we get home."

Kayla shuddered. Who would have thought that after all of this time, it would still feel so new, so fresh? Three years to the day. She had to admit that some days were better than others. In the beginning, it was very rough for her. But other times, she actually could get up enough energy to laugh out loud.

Checking her makeup, she couldn't help but laugh to herself. It was nothing but a dab of lip-gloss but to Kayla, it seemed like much more. Making sure that she hadn't smeared on too much, she rushed out to her car.

Jennifer sat on the bed at Grady Memorial Hospital, shivering and shaking from the coolness of the room. She hated hospitals and avoided them at all costs. Even when she found out that her dad was dying, she refused to come visit him. After all the years that had passed between them, the time had finally come when he was actually going to die. At one time in her life, she couldn't wait for the day. Yet on this day, she sat in very same emergency room that he was in. "God, how could you be so cruel?" she thought.

Jennifer remembered the day so clearly when she last saw her dad. He had just returned from one of his drinking fests at about 4:00 in the morning. Jennifer's mom had been up all night pacing back and forth calling on the Lord to bring him home safely. They had recently had an argument about God knows what. He had just cursed her for the umpteenth time and smacked her around. Yet, through a busted lip and a swollen eye, Jennifer watched her mom pray that he would return to her.

"Why do you want him to come back home? So he could bust your ass again?"

Jennifer thought about the obscenities that she had yelled at her mom and felt immediate remorse as she sat on the bed. Even seven years later. At that tender age of sixteen, Jennifer had developed a tough exterior. Maybe it was due to the changes that she was going through on her journey to womanhood or maybe it was because of the hell that she felt that she was living in. Either way, at that time, she did not care as the words came hurling out of her mouth.

"Jennifer Lynn Mitchell, don't you dare curse me. That is your father whether you like it or not. And he is my husband. I love him and this is his home, do you hear me."

"Yeah, I hear you all right. But I am not listening. Mama, I can't keep watching him hurt you like this. Hmmph, I won't ever let some man hit me just because he's my husband. If you know like I know, I won't ever get married either. It is just too much drama anyway."

Jennifer's mom looked at her. "Child, if I have ever taught you one thing, that is to not ever say "never." Do you think I like this? Do you think that I want you to see me like this? Of course not, but baby, he is my husband and I love him. There will be a day when you are going to love someone too, and I pray that you never go through this."

Jennifer looked at her mom and felt the rift widen between them. "How dare you tell me that I am going to go through this type of hell for some man? Daddy must have really knocked something loose this time. Before I ever let some man hit on me, I'll kill him first."

No sooner had these thoughts entered her mind, Jennifer heard the key turn in the lock. Her dad, Willie Lee Mitchell, walked through the door. Wherever he had been for the past few hours seemed to sober him up. "Hey baby, why are you still up?" He spoke to her mom. "Jennifer, why aren't you in the bed?" Jennifer just looked up at him with disgust. *He always has to come in here with that Baby crap as if that's going to make things right. Her mama was a grown woman, not some two-year old. Or was she?* Jennifer looked over at her mom and almost choked. Her mom looked as if she was relishing in her position of being Daddy's little girl again.

"I'm outta here." Jennifer announced with all the power she could possess.

"Outta where?" Jennifer's dad asked.

"I'm leaving."

"Child, where in the world do you think you are going to go. You are sixteen years old."

"Anywhere is better than here." Jennifer looked straight at her mom.

"Ann," Jennifer's dad looked to her mom, "you better talk some sense into this child of yours. Shoot, I'm getting ready to go to bed. My head is pounding right now. Y'all two need to get yourselves together, you hear."

She watched as her dad strolled out of the living room.

"So, missy, you think that you are so grown that you can make it on your own."

"I'll do my best. Anything would be better than staying in this hell. I refuse to sit back and watch him beat you again and again. And you do absolutely nothing about it. I have never ever seen you raise a hand to him or even tell him to stop. I am not going to sit around here and watch you die."

Jennifer marched into her bedroom and grabbed the suitcase that she kept packed out of her closet. Something in her spirit always told her to save any money that she received from birthdays or babysitting jobs. She counted her stash and saw that she had well over $1000. At her age, you would have assumed that she thought that amount was a fortune. But Jennifer was well beyond her years. She knew that $1000 would get her only but so far. She needed another way to survive.

Jennifer marched back into the living room and out the front door, never hearing her mother say, "I'm already dead."

Back in the hospital bed, past memories began to flood her mind. She had definitely found another way to survive. That's how she ended up in the very predicament that she was in. Being out on her own was like an adventure for Jennifer at first. She was able to move in with her best friend and her mom. Thank goodness, Alicia had been there for her. Many nights, Jennifer had found refuge at their home. Being a single parent, Mrs. Adams was all too aware of its hardships but she never seemed to let it get her down. She spent most of her time going between work and church. She also made sure to bring Alicia up with a faith that was too strong for Jennifer to understand. There were times when Jennifer would look at her friend as if she had three heads. Was she that naïve that she did not know what life was truly like? Poor girl, she didn't understand reality at all. Alicia always seemed to think that God was going to make a way.

"Hmmph, if that was so true then why did he give me the parents that I had," Jennifer thought.

Jennifer was able to stay with the Adamses until she finished high school. It was cool for a while but she always knew that there would be a time when she would have to leave. Ms. Adams always made it clear that she was more than welcome to stay and go on off to college with Alicia. But Jennifer refused. What was going to college going to prove? Her own mother went to college and ended up with a life that was filled with disappointment and pain. Jennifer decided to not even waste her time.

While Alicia headed off to college, Jennifer stayed right in Atlanta. She was able to land a job in the medical field and made a decent living as a dental assistant. Considering she hadn't gone to college, she had done very well for herself. She secured an apartment in Stone Mountain and even brought a car. Everything was finally falling into place for her. She had an apartment, job, and a car. The only thing she was missing from this American dream was a man to share it all with.

"Oh my goodness, I know that I didn't just say that I needed a man." For the past few years, Jennifer avoided men at all cost. Yes, she was attracted to them and everything. There was no doubt about that. But maintaining a relationship with them was another thing all together. She dated every so often but it was nothing that she cared to write home about or share with her best friend.

She and Alicia talked on the phone every weekend. Alicia always had a story to share about some guy she met while Jennifer always talked about work.

"Girl, when are you going to get a man?" Alicia asked.

"Who me? I don't think so. Can't no man do for me what I can do for myself," Jennifer flippantly answered. "Besides, what happened to your holier than thou attitude. You know, your mama will flip out if she knew you were dating around."

"Don't you know that I know," Alicia answered. "Just make sure you don't tell her anything. You know, she has a way of pulling everything up out of you, especially, after feeding you her peach cobbler."

"Who you tellin'. Your mom still gets over on me all the time. But I have a plan for her today. When I go over there, I just won't eat anything. In fact, I'll pick up a bagel first to put in my stomach so I won't be so hungry when I get there."

"Girl, please. You can eat twenty bagels and still have room for her peach cobbler."

"I know, I know."

The two women laughed.

"Well, I think that it is time for me to go right now. I could swear that I smell her cobbler," Jennifer inhaled deeply.

"See, that's not fair. I should be eating it and not you," Alicia answered.

"You're right about that. But you were the one who decided to go off to school. I knew what I was doing when I said that I was going to stay near home."

"Very funny. Very funny. I'll talk to you later," Alicia quipped.

"Sounds like a plan. Bye-bye."

Jennifer walked over to Mrs. Adams' house. She was sitting out on the porch sipping on some tea.

"Hey, baby. I'm glad that you made it. You know, I was getting worried about you."

"Ma Bay, you know that I wouldn't miss dinner with you. I live for these times," Jennifer jokingly answered.

"Yeah, you do. But for how long?"

"Ma Bay, what are you talking about? "I plan on doing this forever."

"Uh-hmm, that is until you meet some man."

"Well that won't happen for a while, I promise you that. I never plan on giving this up."

"Lordy, lordy, lordy. I knew the day was coming," Mrs. Adams replied while looking up to the heavens. "Please watch over her."

"Ma Bay, what are you talking about?"

"Chile, don't you know that you should never ever say *never*. That only gives the devil permission to come into your life."

Jennifer looked at her surrogate mom with disbelief. Did she not just utter the same words that her mom said the very day that she walked out of her home?

"I'm sorry, Ma Bay. But I have to disagree with you here. I plan on eating with you like this for the rest of my life and ain't no devil in hell going to stop me."

Ma Bay began to shake her head but she didn't utter a word. She reached out and touched Jennifer on her forehead.

"Lord, in the name of Jesus, cover this child with your blood. Let no hurt, harm, or danger come to her. Keep her Lord as she goes out on this journey in life."

Jennifer knew not to pull away from Ma Bay when she prayed over her. In fact, she couldn't if she wanted to. There was a part of her that knew that Ma Bay's very prayers were what had brought her this far.

"OK, baby, come on into the kitchen and get some food. I made your favorites."

"That's good to know because I don't even know what my favorites are."

Jennifer walked into the kitchen and sat down at the table. She and Ma Bay ate in silence for the first time in years. No one uttered a word. Never did she know that this would be their last time to dine together, their last supper.

Tears began to fill the corners of Jennifer's eyes as she remembered. What had happened to her in the past six months, she could not explain. She was still in shock about everything.

"So, Ms. Mitchell, can you please tell me what happened?"

Jennifer looked at the uniformed woman who stood in front of her. All of her life, she had wanted to call the police when her dad beat her mom, but was always afraid. So why in the world, was she sitting in front of this woman? When did she decide to make the call to 911?

Jennifer closed her eyes to try to stop the flow of tears that had pooled around their edges.

"What am I supposed to say?" she asked.

"Start from the beginning. Tell me what happened to your face."

"My face?"

Jennifer reached up to touch her face and winced from the pain. Her top lip felt as if it weighed about five pounds. Her right eye was oozing some sort of fluid; she wasn't sure if it was blood or tears.

"Who are you?" she asked the uniformed officer.

Although she had previously stated her name to Ms. Mitchell, the officer answered in a calm voice.

"My name is Celeste Conners. I am an officer for the DeKalb Police Department. I work in the Victims Services Department. I was told to report here to get your statement."

"My statement? About what?"

"Ma'am, about your face. You have bruises all over your face. How did you get them?"

"I don't know. I can't remember."

Officer Conners began to get antsy. She had been working in Victims Services for too long. Each time, she would rush over to the hospital to take a victim's statement. And each time, it felt like battle. No one ever wanted to talk. They were always confused. How confused can you be when your nose has been knocked halfway off your face? Someone did this to you and it wasn't the wall; unless of course, you went flying into one after being knocked with a fist.

Officer Conners was pissed off. She had specifically come to this department because she had wanted to make a difference. She had witnessed her very own mom get beat almost every day. She had even buried her very own best friend just a few months ago. Thank God she still had her badge. Thank God, her best friend's husband confessed to everything and was now locked up for a very long time. But Lisa was still gone and would never come back ever.

"Look, Ms. Mitchell. I am going to say some things to you right now. And I am going to tell you that it is not as a police officer but as a woman. And while I talk to you, I am going to give you this mirror to look into."

Officer Conners knew that she was about to cross the line at that moment and didn't care one iota.

She handed Jennifer the mirror and began speaking.

"My name right now is not Officer Conners but it is Celeste. You can call me Celeste. I need to say this to you, so please listen. I have grown up in a household that was filled with rage, hatred, and chaos. I watched my mother get beat everyday of my life."

Jennifer looked at the officer at that moment as she continued.

"I just buried my best friend a few months ago. Her husband finally kept his promise. Each time she went back to him, he promised that he would never hit her again. And each time he continued to do so. They went back in forth for years through this game. I talked to her. Her family talked to her. But each time, she went back hoping that he would fulfill his promise. And you know what, he finally came through. He will never hit her one more time because he killed her."

Jennifer looked at the officer as tears dripped down her uniform.

"So you see, I made a vow to myself that I would not let another woman die because of unfulfilled promises. I made my own promise. Now, as an officer, I am not allowed to tell you what to do in any way. But as a woman, I have to let you know that the only way you can go is down. I want you to look at yourself in that mirror and tell yourself, not me, that you don't know what happened to your face. I want you to tell yourself that everything is just fine."

Officer Conners took the mirror out of Jennifer's lap and held it in front of her face. Jennifer looked into the mirror and took a gasp. Her mother. She looked just like her mother did on the day that she walked out of her life. Through swollen tear stained eyes, and a busted lip, Jennifer spoke.

"He did this to me."

"Who did this to you?"

"My boyfriend, Jason."

"But why? What happened?"

"I don't know what happened. It's never been like this before. Never this bad."

"Well, each time, it will get worse and worse."

"I know, I know. But I love him. He says that he loves me. He's all I got."

"I know you feel that way. But let me tell you this. When I last spoke with my best friend, I told her that I could not sit around any longer and watch her die. How could she expect me too?"

Her words registered in Jennifer's spirit. "I said the same thing to my mom when I left home."

"So, tell me what happened." Officer Conners asked.

"I refused to stay around and haven't looked back since." Jennifer answered

"So, what do you think that this is saying to you right now?"

"It's saying that I should not sit around and watch my own self die."

"Now you have a way out, Jennifer. That is if you want to take it. There is a place that you can go. As a matter of fact, it just opened today. I know the director personally. Give me the go ahead and I will take you there myself. What do you say?"

Jennifer looked at herself in the mirror.

"I say "I'm outta here. Let's do this."

Officer Conners spoke, "Let me make some phone calls and I will be right back."

"Ok, I'll be here," Jennifer answered.

"Where else do I have to go," Jennifer whispered to herself as Officer Conners exited. "I'm already dead."

When Officer Conners arrived back into the hospital room, Jennifer was still sitting in the same place staring off into the distance. "Oh, my God, Lis…" Officer Conners saw her very own best friend sitting on the hospital bed. Lisa would always seem to be looking off to some faraway place. "A penny for your thoughts," Celeste would always ask.

"Girl, I am about to make you a millionaire because my head is full of many thoughts. Why, Celeste, tell me why I can't leave him for good?"

"It's because you love him, baby. It's as simple as that."

"But it's wrong. Look at me, I am a mess. My body's messed up, my mind is messed up. I can't think straight anymore and I am hurting way down inside my soul."

"I know you are. I am hurting also. I see you and what you are going through. And you know that you are my girl. If I could, I would take you away now. But I also know that this is a decision that only you can make. When you get tired enough, then you will leave for good."

"But when will I get tired enough?"

"I don't know. Only God knows. But one thing I do know is that I can't continue to see you knowing that it might be my very last time."

"I'm so sorry Celeste. I know that I am hurting you. My mom and dad are completely beside themselves with worry. They are so sick and tired of me going back and forth. I swear I don't know when my time will be up either. Sometimes it seems as if I am dead right now."

"Girl, you need to stop tripping. You are not dead. Your body is right here in front of me."

"You don't understand what I mean. My body may be here but my soul is gone."

Celeste felt a chill run through her spine. She looked at her best friend and finally understood. She was dead. In order to go through the hell that she was living, there was no way that she could not be. Her eyes held a blank stare. But for how long?

"Lisa, how long? I'm sorry. How long? Celeste began to babble. "I never noticed. I never noticed."

"Girl, please. How many people take the time to really look at another person? To see if there is joy, life, in their eyes. Not too many, for sure. Do you know why? As long as we say that things are cool with us, then that's enough. As long as we pretend that life is grand, then everything is just fine. That's that surface thing happening. But what happens when you decide to listen a little harder, or look a little deeper. Then you start to see things that were once hidden, and these things may not be so pretty. Then, it means you might have to do something, be accountable to them and to yourself. Be accountable to God, you know what I am saying."

"And speaking of God, what do you think about Him?" Celeste interjected.

"I don't know. Up until this point I did not really think about Him. There was a time when I cried out to Him to help me, save me, and take me from my situation. But it was if He didn't hear me. Yes, I would leave but I always ended up going back there. It was so hard to make it on my own."

Somehow, Celeste found herself listening for the first time. "Lisa, you say that you asked God to take you from the situation."

"Yeah, I did."

"But did you ask him to come into your heart and renew your mind and spirit. I mean, you only asked him for just a little bit and he came through, he made a way for you to get out each time, yet your old mindset continued to bring you back. So it wasn't God's fault. He only does what we allow Him to do." Celeste felt as if she was pulling at straws because she had never spoken of the Lord.

"Wow, girl, that was deep. I never looked at it this way. In all of this time, I guess I was angry because I thought that God had forgotten about me, you know. I wanted him to come in and fix my problems for me but I can see now that he just wants to fix me."

"Yes, that's right. Look at it this way, you say that you are dead but you know like I know that God is in the life giving business. Ask him to come into you heart and mind and see what happens."

"Come on now, Celeste. Do you think that all I need to do is open myself up to God and he will make it all better, just like that?"

Not sure of where this was going, but knowing that something was definitely happening at that very moment, Celeste's faith began to grow. God had to do something because her best friend was hanging on to the very last thread.

"Yes, I believe that this is all that you have to do. Give it all up to God and He will handle the rest."

"Ok, now. I am going to believe just like you." Lisa began to speak. "God, it's me. You know, Lisa. God, I am hurting right now and I don't know where else to turn. I need You Lord. I need You to come into my life and make me over. God, I can't continue to go through the fighting and the pain. I can't continue to let Ryan do this to me. You would never hurt me. You love me Lord, You love me just as I am. In all of my craziness, You still love me... Oh, my God, You love *me* Lord. Thank you Lord. Thank you Lord."

Celeste listened as her best friend spoke. She understood. Lisa really understood that the Lord still loved her and will always love her.

"Girl, He loves me, of all people. Even with all of my junk, He still loves me."

"Yes, he does, Lisa. He loves you and I love you. We just want you to love yourself just as much as we do."

"But how, how can I love myself knowing all that I have done?"

"You love yourself the way that God loves you and all of those things will pass away."

"You know what, Celeste. In just that short moment, I felt them going away. I felt God coming all up in me, you know."

"I know you did, and so did I."

"So what else do I need to say?"

"It's not what you say, it's what you believe. Do you believe that God sent his only son Jesus to come into your life?"

"Yes."

"Do you believe that he died on the cross for you and me?"

"Yes."

"Do you believe that he was buried and rose from the dead so that you may have life?"

"Yes."

"Do you believe that all of your sins are forgiven? Do you believe that by his stripes you are healed?"

"Yes, yes."

"Well, then baby, you are saved, for real this time."

"I am? I am. I am." Each time Lisa spoke with more confidence. In herself and in the Lord.

"Well, Celeste, I don't even know if you know the impact that you have had on my life at this moment. But I am finished. I have turned everything over to God, completely. I don't know what's going to happen next, but I do know that He has my back."

Celeste looked at her girl and felt her heart quicken. Bleakness and despair fled from her eyes and joy and assurance had now taken up residence.

"So it is time for me to go on home now."

"Go home? What do you mean, go home."

"Girl, I got some unfinished business to take care of but don't you worry about me. My home is not with Ryan."

"Don't leave now. Just hang out here and we'll check out a few movies."

"No can do. I have to go now before I change my mind."

Sure enough, Lisa walked out of Celeste's house for the very last time. No sooner had she gotten into her car and drove away did Ryan pull up next to her and shoot her. Her best friend was gone immediately.

The next few months were a blur. Celeste took a few weeks off from work but had no idea what she did. Lisa's funeral was a complete blank. Everyone tried to offer their condolences but Celeste didn't hear their words. She slept in the day and was wide awake at night. Her world was completely upside down. That was until the night of July 17. Celeste has dozed off to sleep on the living room couch after crying her eyes out. She kept replaying the last time when she and Lisa talked in her kitchen. "God, I should have stopped her. I should have made her sit down. Why didn't I make her stay?"

That's when she heard a small voice say, "Because you weren't supposed to. You did all that you were supposed to."

"How could you say that? My friend is dead."

"That's where you're wrong. Your friend was already dead. She told you that herself. But you helped bring her back to life, you helped bring her back to me."

"I did?"

"Yea, girl you did" Celeste heard Lisa's voice as if she was sitting next to her.

"Lisa, is that you?"

"In the flesh, hahaha. Yes, it's me. Celeste, you gave me my life back right there in your kitchen."

"But how? How did I do that when you lost it outside of my door?"

"I didn't lose my life. I gave it up to God in the kitchen. He just tucked it away for safekeeping."

"I don't get it, I don't understand."

"Remember when I told you that I needed to go home, I meant that I needed to go back to God. I also said that I had to go before I changed my mind. Girl, I couldn't stay any longer. Ryan was going to kill me. I knew that, you knew that, my family knew that too. It was inevitable. Our situation was too volatile. It was a matter of time. But God was able to use you to bring me to Him so that that my soul would not be lost. The joy that came into my life when I gave my life to Christ in your kitchen was the same joy that was in my soul when Ryan pulled the trigger. I knew that God already had my back and I was ready to let go and go to Him."

"But, it's not fair. I lost you in the whole process. You're not here anymore."

"No I am not there in the flesh, but my spirit will always be with you. And girl, you know that you shouldn't be so selfish either. If I had stayed with you, who knows how long it would have taken before Ryan would have tried to make me lose my mind. Girl, I wasn't in the best frame of mind, you know that."

"But…"

"But, nothing. It was my time and I thank you for leading me back to the Lord. Now, if you want really want to do something, why don't you think of ways that you can help all those other women who are going through the same abuse that I went through. Find a way to help them get out and stay out. I'm not saying that you should kill them or anything like that…"

"Lisa, how could you say that?"

"Girl, please you know that I am just tripping. We do have a sense of humor up here. But for real, you say that you did not want me to die but you wanted me to live right."

"Yes."

"Well, why don't you help these women live a life without fear, abuse, and pain? Help them find a way to love themselves again."

That very day was the day that Celeste vowed that she would do all that she could to help those very women who were living defeated lives. Although she was limited in her resources, it wasn't too long before God began to do his thing.

Sharee sat on the living room couch in utter shock. She could not believe that he did it again. How could he? How could he do it to her again?

The telephone receiver lying sprawled across floor was evidence that she had reached her limit. It had been shattered into many tiny pieces after being thrown across the room. Everything happened so quickly. She never thought that she could get so angry. Usually Robert was the one to throw a tantrum or have a fit. But not Sharee. She hated fighting. She hated arguing. But a rage seemed to come out of nowhere and she could not control it even if she wanted to. She was tired, bone tired. Everything hurt on her body. Her head hurt from all the tormenting thoughts and images that rolled around in her mind. Her throat hurt was raw from all the screaming she had done. And her heart felt as if it was being torn from each artery, one vessel at a time. This was the last straw. Robert had really crossed the line this time. There was no way that he could lie his way out of this one.

After all of the years that they had spent together, Sharee never thought that it would end this way. She and Robert had their share of drama for the past 14 years. The love of her life, her first love. Sharee thought that she and Robert would be together for years. In fact, as more people wagered their longevity, Sharee vowed that she would prove them wrong. She knew Robert had his ways, all men did. She was well aware that he may have cheated on her a few times, but what man doesn't cheat. She even knew that he might not have loved her as much as she loved him, but that was still OK. Whether it was true or not, it didn't matter because Robert always came back home.

But this phone call was so different from the last. Sharee was always used to hearing a woman's voice on the other end professing her love for Robert. She was even used to finding out that there might have even been a love child involved in the brief affair. But the operative word was brief. Things never lasted too long. Robert could always refute everything that was said. He always had an excuse that Sharee didn't necessarily want to believe but found that it was easier than losing him. Besides, she wasn't really suffering as badly as most woman. Robert took care of the household with no problem and always made sure that Sharee had anything her heart desired. Everything that is, except himself.

Sharee didn't mind putting up with things. Hmmph, on the outside, everyone constantly praised his and her relationship. Here she was with a man who took care of home. Her girl friends made sure to let her know. Sharee could work if she wanted to or she could take it easy. Robert was some kind of eye candy. He had it going on, you hear.

Sharee had to admit that she was all caught up into Robert, too. She thought about the first time when she spoke to him. Who would have thought that she would have ever gotten up the nerve to say anything back to him? She had watched him for several weeks whenever he came into her office. Working as a receptionist at Walker and Raines Marketing firm gave her the opportunity to observe all the clients who came looking for the right words, right strategies that could take their business to new heights. She was always amazed at the transformation that developed after they finished their first consultation. A gleam of hope sparkled in their eyes from their new revelation.

But, meeting Robert was so opposite. He came in the door already full of confidence and she found herself wondering why he was even there. Each week, he would stop by her desk and spark up conversation with her. "Today's a beautiful day, isn't it?" he asked.

"Yes it is. Yes it is."

"You know, it's almost as beautiful as you are" Robert quickly added.

Sharee was taken aback. Did he just compliment me? she asked to herself.

Robert stared at Sharee and waited for her response.

"Hmm, why thank you. I didn't expect to hear that."

"I didn't expect to say it; however, I could not help myself. You are very beautiful." Silence took a stand between the two.

"I am usually not this forward. However, I cannot help myself. Would you like to join me for dinner today? Nothing too fancy or expensive. Just a simple place to meet and talk. What do you say?"

Sharee realized that she had not gone out on a date in years. She resounded herself to her work and home.

Without exuding the desperation she felt, she answered "Why yes, I would love to have dinner with you."

Robert passed her his business card and left.

Sharee sat at her desk, mentally planning her outfit and hairstyle for the evening. Never realizing that she did not know where they were going and when.

"Hmmph, I guess desperation was written on my forehead after all because from that one date, Robert has taken me on a journey that has kept me guessing and left in the dark for way too long." Sharee began to pry through Robert's items. She never thought that she would be reduced to snooping like Sherlock Holmes but she needed to find evidence to show Robert. He would easily refute her claim unless she had something concrete. Robert always had a way of saying that every insecurity, accusation, and irrational thought was a figment of her imagination.

As she searched the house, bits and pieces of the phone conversation replayed in her ears.

We were together for several years.

"I'm gonna kill him. Lord, you better step in right now because one of us is going to die today." Sharee found herself screaming throughout the house. The house that was supposed to bring her joy only reverberated the echoes of her voice. Sharee went from room to room. The guest bedroom, immaculately designed with creams, golds, and yellows, looked like it had been touched by the sun's rays. Yet, it was destroyed as if a mighty wind had come through. The master bedroom, decorated in royal purple and blue, was supposed to be their haven, their love nest. Unfortunately, there was always something amiss. Could it have been love? There was a cold eerie draft where there should have been warmth and desire.

Sharee continued to run through the house, overturning every thing that crossed her path.

Ring. Ring. Ring.

"What was that noise?"

Ring Ring Ring.

"What now? Are they calling back because they forgot to lodge the last knife into her soul?"

Sharee picked up the phone in a huff.

"Why do you keep calling me? Leave me alone."

The other voice answered, "Leave you alone. What are you talking about? Sharee, Is that you?"

Sharee began twisting the phone cord around her arm. Each twist muffled her cries.

"Sharee, baby. You are making me very nervous. Are you there? Sharee, is Robert there? Girl, I'm coming over."

Sharee looked at the videotape repeatedly, always rewinding to that spot, the precise spot 1:20:43. Sharee collapsed on the floor and waited for her best friend to arrive.

Although Robert and Sharee were married for over fourteen years, Kayla still had the key to their home. Sharee had given it to her after their honeymoon in Aruba with the only stipulation. It was to be used for emergency use only. Sharee would always say, "Girl, if you ever have any inkling that Robert is cutting up and my life is on the line, you better use this key. I don't care where we are. You better come and get me."

Kayla rang the doorbell and there was no answer. She dialed her friend's number from her cell phone. Still no response.

"Bump that. I'm going in."

"Sharee," she yelled, "It's me, girl. Here I come. Make a noise of something to tell me where you are," Kayla yelled.

"To tell me that you are alive. Please don't be dead'" she whispered. Fear began to wrap itself around Kayla. The silence of the house was deafening. Not knowing where to go, she found herself heading straight for the den.

There she saw her best friend of twenty years lying in a heap amidst broken glass and strewn clothes.

"Oh, my God. Sharee. Are you bleeding? What did Robert do to you? Where is he?"

Sharee could not talk. She couldn't even hold her head up.

"Baby, I love you" Kayla heard in the background. Expecting to see Robert and Sharee, Kayla turned around towards the sound. Kayla's bottom jaw dropped. As she viewed the video, her stomach turned. Robert wasn't confessing his love to Sharee, instead it was to his best friend, Carter. Although they had not grown up together, Carter and Robert had developed a close friendship with one another within the last few years. As far as Kayla knew, Sharee was as comfortable with the relationship as ever and did not feel threatened in the least.

"Sharee, what in the world is going on?"

"I don't know. I don't know. I received a phone call from Carter this morning. He was telling me that he could not keep this secret any longer."

"So what are you saying?"

"Exactly what I just said. Carter and Robert aren't just close friends, they are *together*."

"Girl, you need to stop lying. Come on now, Robert has done some low down things in the past but this is ridiculous. I don't believe you."

"Kayla, are you blind. Didn't you hear him? "*Baby I love you.*" What kind of B S is that?"

"Men can say I love you, just like women. What's so wrong with that?"

"Kayla, he didn't just say I love you, he said, *Baby* I love you. What man in his right mind would call his boy, Baby? Now I know we have that Cash Money guy, but let's be for real. It's not natural."

"I don't know. I cannot believe it. So what did Carter say about all of this? "

"He said that he was sorry to have kept this a secret for so long but his conscience was eating him up. They were only together a few times and it has been years since then. After he had gotten to know me, he realized that it was totally wrong. Ain't that some crap? What if he hadn't like me so much, would this have gone on today."

"I still don't understand. In all the years that Robert has slipped out the back door, there have only been women calling you. You never received a phone call from a dude."

"I know I haven't. But that just shows you how trifling Robert is. But don't you worry about it. I have a trick for his ass." Sharee started straightening her clothing.

"Sharee, what are you going to do? I mean, come on now. You put up with his cheating all of these years when you thought it was with women, but now, you are plotting and planning to destroy him because of a man. Cheating is cheating."

"Kayla, you just don't get it. When Robert was cheating with all of those women, it bothered me, don't get it twisted. However, I still had the opportunity to compete. I could work on myself. But how in the world am I supposed to compete with a man. If Robert had given me the inkling that he was swinging both ways then I could have decided if I wanted to be bothered in all of that drama. He never gave me the opportunity to choose my fate."

"Choose your fate. What kind of nonsense is that?"

"It's the truth. Women do it all the time. When their men are straight up from the beginning, then the women have the option to fool with them or throw them to the curb."

"So you mean to tell me that if Robert told you that he preferred men and women, then you would have been down."

"I'm not saying that. It's just that he lied to me. Our whole life has been one big lie"

"What I don't understand is why Carter said something now. He even admitted that there has been years since then."

"I tried to ask him about that and he kept saying that nothing was going on now but he could not rest. His conscience wouldn't allow him to. Since he started going to church, he needed to confess all of his sins. Hmmph, I think that this is something that he should have kept to himself."

"Do you mean to tell me that you would prefer to be kept in the dark about something this serious? Especially in this day and age. What about your health?"

"I know. It's just that I may be able to handle this much better if Robert would have come clean in the first place."

"I understand that. So what are you going to do?"

"I've thought about it. I'm just going to wait here for Robert so that we can *talk*."

Kayla looked at her best friend and knew that talking was the last thing on her mind. Sharee was beyond pissed because not only had Robert played her for a fool. She had to live with the embarrassment that her husband didn't just want her. Sharee began to clench her fingers.

"Sharee, baby. Why don't you take a breather for the day? Or better yet for the next few days."

"Kayla, what do you mean a breather? Girl, I can barely catch my breath. I feel as if the life has been knocked out of me."

"I understand, Sweetie. But to be honest with you, I know that look. You are about to raise hell all up through here. Now, as much as I understand your rage, there is no way that I am going to allow you to do this. Take a few days off before you speak to Robert. You still need to hear his side of the story."

"There is no *his* side. I just cannot believe that Carter would make up such a lie."

Kayla was feeling exasperated because she knew Sharee like the back of her hand. Sharee doesn't do well with embarrassment and this was surely an embarrassing moment. Sharee understood the high expectations that everyone placed on her relationship with Robert and she always went above and beyond to make sure that everything was in its place. However, this situation was a tad bit too much.

"Look, Sharee, if this was any other day, I would have on my sweats and would pull my hair back into a ponytail. However, I can't do that today. The Soul is opening up today and I need to be there. If you could just hold off for a day or two before confronting Robert, I would feel so much better. You know like I know that I can't possibly concentrate if you are not in place.

Sharee looked over at her friend and saw the anguish that was in her eyes. Knowing that this grand opening meant so much to Kayla, there was no way that Sharee would every dream of spoiling it.

"So what do you say," Kayla asked. "Why don't you come and spend time with me at the Soul. I need you there with me."

"Kayla, I am sure that you can handle it today. I'll just be in the way." Sharee wanted to be alone on this moment.

"No, no, you will not be in the way. In fact, you can help me out. I am so nervous about today. What am I supposed to say to help these women, the ones who have been hurt and are still hurting? Who am I?"

"Who are you? Are you crazy? You are a blessing, not just to those women who come into your center, but to me. There have been times when I have had to ask myself how I could have possibly gone through all that you have and still smile. Kayla, Tyson hit you with his car, not once, but twice. Yet, you are still here. I never could understand why you never even bought charges against his raggedy ass. Instead, you walked away from everything that you had built. Tell me, what was your secret?"

"There was no secret. I had to walk away, better yet, run away. I was so afraid. When I think about his face behind the wheel, I still get chills. Although he was smiling at me, his eyes told a different story."

"You know that you do not have to tell me anything if this is too hard for you." Sharee spoke. In all the years that Kayla had known Sharee, they never discussed the specifics of Kayla's abuse. Sharee just knew that it was bad.

"I know." Kayla looked off into the distance. "Just so you know, him hitting me with the car was the last straw. There were other things that I never shared with anyone. It's too embarrassing."

"Do you want to talk about it now?" Sharee asked, unsure if she really wanted to know.

"No. But hey, I came over here ready to help you, and now we're talking about me. Sharee, you cannot possibly believe that Robert likes men."

"Although I would love to say it cannot be possible, now that I look at things differently, I realize that it could be possible."

"How do you come to that conclusion?"

"It's been a long time since we have been intimate, and to be honest, I really do not care. Each time that we are together, I feel empty and alone."

"Sharee, maybe you and Robert are just going through a dry period. It happens, you know."

"I've felt that also. I have to admit that I was somewhat suspect many times before but always chose to let it go."

"Why do you say that?"

"Robert has always been out there. I would always joke about him and call him a freak. I knew he loved all kinds of women. But there was a part of me that chose not to care or make an issue of it because he chose to marry me. Of all the women that he knew, he chose to marry me."

"You act like Robert did you a favor when he married you. Don't you realize that you are a great catch for any man?"

"I didn't want just any man, I wanted Robert. Girl, I felt like I hit the jackpot."

"Up until now, I felt that you did too. Look, let's just pray that everything will work out for the best."

"Do you always believe that things will work out for the best? How can you be so optimistic?"

"I don't know. I truly believe that God orders each of our footsteps. This situation, as crazy as it seems, has been orchestrated by the Lord himself. Maybe He's telling you that it's time to stop selling yourself short."

"I feel so stupid."

"But remember that you are not stupid. Robert deceived you when he never confessed his alternative lifestyle. He put you in some serious danger."

"Yes he did and payback is a …."

"Don't you dare say it."

"I won't. But what I will do is pack up a few clothes so that I can leave out with you."

"So you are really going to come."

"Yes, I am. There is no way that I can even think of not sharing in this big event with you. Give me a few moments and I will be right back."

Jaynie cowered in the corner by the door. "James, please let me go."

"No, I am not letting you go anywhere until we talk."

"There's nothing to talk about. I am leaving. I asked you to go but you refused."

"You damn right, I did refuse. How in the hell are you going to ask me to leave my own home?"

"But we cannot keep living like this. It's not right."

"So what. I don't care. We are going to talk whether you like it or not. Do you think I am going to let you take my son and walk away from me? Are you crazy? I'll die before that happens."

Jaynie never thought that James would have her backed into the corner. They had been back together for two years now and he never raised his hands to her. But something in her soul told her that things were different at this moment. James was desperate. She saw it in his eyes; she smelled it in the air. Fear had crept back into her soul and taken residence once again.

"Lord, help me," she prayed silently.

"Bitch, after all the time that I invested in you, you think that you are going to up and leave me again. You have a lot of nerve. You know damn well, you weren't shit when I met you and you still aren't. Aint' no man going to want your dumb ass."

"Well then, if that's the case then let me go," Jaynie pleaded.

"No, I ain't letting you go anywhere. Now, whatchu gonna do about that?"

At that moment, Jaynie needed to make a decision. "God, am I supposed to die like this? You told me to go home, Lord, but why?"

Don't worry. I am here with you. Don't back down.

"James, I am going to ask you one more time, please let me go."

"Hell, naw, I ain't letting you go nowhere," James smirked.

Jaynie made a resolution at that moment. "God, if this is how it has to be, then so be it but I am getting out of the house."

James continued to harass Jaynie. "Hmmph, you think your ass is so high and mighty. Playing all that gospel music through here.

Running back and forth to church, taking care of this one and that one. Yet, you think you're too good for me. Packing up your shit in front of me as if I ain't nothing. I am something, I am somebody. You are the one who ain't shit. In case you didn't know it, you definitely ain't no prize."

That was it. Those four little words set off a time bomb in Jaynie. "I ain't no prize. What?" Jaynie leaped up and reached out straight for James' jugular. "I ain't no prize. Nigga, I will kill you." She began squeezing harder. James weighed over 200 pounds, yet, at that moment he felt as light as a feather.

God what's going on. Lord what am I doing?

Jaynie watched the whole scenario from a bird's eye view as James' body was pushed across the kitchen floor.

Run, girl, run

Jaynie began to run through the living room and out the front door. As she ran towards her car, she saw her son Lance. At fourteen years old, he was already taller than her by three inches, however, at that moment, he looked as if he was only five years old.

"Get in the car, Lance. Now!" Jaynie whispered.

How he heard her, only God knows, but Lance got in the car just as Jaynie approached it. Getting in, she locked the doors just as James reached the window.

"Get out of the fucking car, Jaynie." James yelled

"Lance, baby. Stop crying."

Jaynie backed the car out of the driveway as best as she could.

"Mommy, did he hit you. If he hit you, mommy, I am going to fuck him up. Did he hit you mommy?"

"No baby, he did not hit me. I choked him."

Jaynie continued to drive. It hurt like hell to see Lance crying. "It's all my fault. I should have never come back."

Honk. Honk. Honk. A horn began blowing behind them. James was following them along Lawrenceville Highway.

"Stop the car, Jaynie."

Jaynie stuck up her middle finger and kept driving. "Think. think." *Find a safe place to go.* "Ok, baby, we are going to drive to the police station."

Lance continued to stare off into space. "Mommy, he lied. Mommy, he lied."

"I know baby. He had me fooled, too."

Jaynie began to think about the past twelve years of her life. James and Jaynie were together for 6 years before they separated. Although they never married, very few could distinguish differences between their life and those of married couples. Living the American dream, they now owned a four bedroom ranch in one of Atlanta's suburbs. Although it wasn't as fancy as many of the homes in Gwinnett County, it meant just as much because Jaynie and James had both worked really hard to buy it. Yet, at that moment, Jaynie realized their house was never a home. In fact, it was simply a shell that helped to mask the chaos that was inside.

When did things change for the worse or were they ever good. Jaynie began to question her whole life. When Jaynie left James in 2000, she was at her worse. After enduring many years of name calling and insults, jumping through hoops, and suffering physical abuse at the hands of James, Jaynie finally reached out to the counseling ministry of her church.

February 9, 2000 was the day that would forever change her life. New Hope of Life Missionary Church was offering classes to its members for the upcoming spring semester. A variety of classes were offered whose sole purpose was to lift up the members of the church in every area. Financial planning, entrepreneurial courses, self-improvement classes. As Jaynie browsed through the catalog, she waited along with others in the chapel as each leader explained their class' purpose and mission.

The counseling ministry covered a wide range of areas. The men of Brothers Helping Brothers supported one another as members overcame many issues that affect men, such as, alcoholism, domestic violence, unemployment, and drug addiction. Their leader, Minister Roberts, epitomized the essence of a true man of God. His humility and desire to lead by example was evident by his confident stature. "James needs to be more like him. I might need to pass his number on to James." Jaynie thought. Divorced but Not Destroyed offer support to members who were struggling with moving on after the separation of a spouse. Its mission was to teach members how to find themselves again and move into their divine destiny.

"Ladies and Gentlemen, I would like to introduce the leader of our next group, Women of Destiny." Jaynie watched on as the leader made her way to the podium.

"Good evening, everyone. My name is Minister Kim Alexander and I am part of a wonderful group here at the church."

Jaynie looked on with interest. Minister Alexander seemed to have a glow surrounding her being.

"As I stand before you, I have one mission in mind. That is, to set the captives free. You may say to yourself, *free, I am free* and you may be right. I felt the same way at one point in my life. But I was so wrong. I was locked up, in my mind, in my body, and in my spirit."

"But today," Minister Alexander, "through the grace of God, I am free. Thanks to the group that I am a part of, Women of Destiny. For twenty two years, I was a victim of domestic violence. No, let me change that. I was not a victim. I am a victor. Can I be real with you all please?"

"Amen." "Go for yours." Voices murmured their consent.

Minister Alexander continued. "My husband beat me every other Tuesday. Now, I know that you are all probably thinking that I am lying but believe me, as I stand before God, I am speaking the truth. I know that you are wondering why I let it happen. I can answer that for you. Not only was I locked up in my body, I was also locked up in my mind. I had low self-esteem, was full of fear, and didn't know any better. Literally. Abuse was a part of my bloodline. I watched my mama get beat by my daddy and she watched her mama, my grandma, get beat by my grandfather. All in the name of love. Therefore, I believed that it was OK for love to hurt, even just a little bit. But love is not supposed to hurt. God is love and in the scriptures it says that love is kind. Love is patient."

"Hallelujah. Praise God. Thank you Jesus." Jaynie heard in the background. Audience members were beginning to cheer.

"It wasn't until I realized that my spirit was locked up that I decided to make a change. As I stood in my bathroom, afraid to look at myself in the mirror, I had an encounter with the Lord. And you know what He told me. He said, "You are fearfully and wonderfully made." Hmmph, I thought I had lost my mind. Can I keep it real with you all?"

"You go right ahead."

"Here I was, with bruises all over my body. You see, my husband would beat me but it was never visible. A slap upside the head never left a bruise. A pinch on the inside of my thigh would never be seen by others. The name calling and threats were for my ears only. I was always on the brink of confusion because I know it happened yet I never seemed to have proof. Who would actually believe my word against his? However, his word was not God's word. God's word says in Psalm 139, you are fearfully and wonderfully made."

Jaynie's eyes began to tear up and her body began to feel warm. She too knew about the confusion. James would berate her in public and in private. She didn't know which was worse.

"Yet, on that day," Minister Alexander continued, "there was no confusion. I had not just one black eye, but two. There was no way that I could go into work like that. Many times before, I could explain away the soreness and stiffness. Coworkers would laugh and say, "Girl, your husband must be really putting it down. You can barely walk. Hmmph, I need me someone like that?" If they only knew. If they only knew. He was putting it down all right. He was pushing my spirit down instead of lifting me up. It was if I was the walking dead. God is spirit and I had none."

"But that day, I felt God all through my bathroom and all through my spirit. He made me look in that mirror."

My child, look at yourself. Kimmie, look at yourself. You see, God called me Kimmie. I hadn't heard my nickname as a little girl since my aunt Joann passed away. She was my favorite aunt. She always spoke life into me as a child. *Baby, don't you know God is watching you. He will never forsake you or leave you alone.* I miss her so much. God had to go there and bring her spirit back to me. I guess he knew that I would have dismissed my encounter with Him." Minister Alexander took a deep breath.

"Nevertheless, I looked and there it was. Forget the black eyes, that was minor. I looked into my eyes, into my soul, and saw nothing. For twenty-two years, I was able to endure all that I had because I wasn't there. Thank God, I wasn't an active participant. I never fought back because I thought that this would make it more difficult. It was better to let my husband go through his routine. We had it down to a science, our own special dance."

Jaynie could not believe Minister Alexander was as transparent as this. "I don't think I could ever be so public with my shame."

"Choose this day. Life or death. All of those years I chose death. It was easy to do that. I could sit back and play the victim of my circumstances. I had all the right to. However, to choose life required that I wake up and take a long look at myself. This was not how I dreamed my life to be. But when I think about it. At that time of my life, I was not dreaming. My mind had not yet been transformed. *So as a man thinketh, so is he.* My thinking was only limited to my world, my little box. Yet, dreaming requires that we get in sync with God's thoughts which are greater than we can ever imagine. *My thoughts for you are beautiful."* Minister Alexander began to choke.

"When I think of God's goodness, I cannot help but cry out. Thank you Lord. At one time, I thought that my tears were a sign of weakness. *Look at you, a grown women crying like a baby*, my husband would say to me after one of our Tuesday night smack downs. So I stopped crying. Crying wasn't going to change anything. Yet, as I stood in that bathroom, I began to cry. And it hurt, literally. Crying with a sty is one thing, but crying with a black eye is another. But you know what, I found out later that God bottles each and every one of our tears. Hmmph, I had some tears, you hear me. I began to cry out to my past feelings of hurt, rejection, and loneliness. I was such a lonely child never feeling as if I belonged to anyone. I cried out to my present situation which was full of despair, broken promises, and regret. I cried out to my future because I knew that this was the day when I would finally choose life even though it could lead to my death. Yet the salt from my tears healed me. Salt is a preserver."

"Now, as you can see, I am not dead, thanks to the grace of God. However, I came close. I came out of that bathroom knowing that where I was I could never be and where I was going, I just didn't know. Either way, this was it. I told you earlier that Tuesday was fight night yet today was Wednesday. Don't you know that joy comes in the morning, yes it does. Although I was bruised on the outside, there was a shifting in my spirit from death to life. The hell that I was living in served its purpose. Its heat was so hot and I was getting burned. Yet, the burning helped to burn away all of my fleshly desires and bring me back to my spiritual being."

"If only I could have beamed myself out of my home, but that was not possible. I had to face the consequences of my decision. When my husband woke up the next morning, he was as refreshed as ever. "Good morning, baby. What's for breakfast?" Now, I hadn't cooked a thing for the first time in twenty two years."

"Nothing."

"What do you mean, nothing? I'm hungry."

"Well, I'm not, so therefore I did not cook."

"Oh, you're still tripping from last night. Well I told you that I was sorry. Things just got out of hand. But you shouldn't have tried to step to me like you did."

"Step to you? I was trying to make you stop hitting me. What was I supposed to do?"

"Look, are you going to cook or what?"

Minister Alexander looked into the audience. "Listen yall. I have to admit that I was shocked at my own response. I said to him, "We could go out to get something to eat."

"We can't go anywhere, you know that."

"Why not, we go any other time after one of our fights."

"Well, we can't go today. Look, are you going to cook breakfast or what?"

"No, I want you to tell me why we can't go out to eat."

"Because I said so, that's why. Look at you."

"I have looked at me and I want to go out to eat."

"I'm not going with you anywhere. You are tripping. You need to chill now or…"

"Or what. You might hit me. You might leave me. You might kill me. Hmmph, which one? You don't want the neighbors to see what goes on behind closed doors. Are you embarrassed? Any other time, we can conceal everything but its kind of hard to do that with two black eyes. With one black eye, I could get an eye patch, cover it up, and say that I have pink eye. I can try it with two eye patches, cover them up, and say that I was blind. Which wouldn't be a lie? I was blinded by you."

"Who do you think you are talking too?"

"I am talking to you. I have already said it. I want to go out to eat. I ain't ashamed, what about you? Are you ashamed?" Minister Alexander stopped speaking and stared at the audience. "Listen yall. I put on my coat and headed straight for the door. I didn't know where I was going or what I was doing yet I could not stop myself."

"Look, Kim, I am not playing around. You better not go out that door."

"I turned the handle just as my husband tried to grab me. Hmmph, I was quick. I walked out of my house and stood at that foot of my driveway. As my neighbors came out to get there mail, I greeted them with the biggest hello. Many of them looked at me strangely, yet not one asked me what happened or if I needed help. Now, I know that you are all probably wondering where my husband was in all of this. Let me tell you, he was still in the house. Afraid to come out and face the world. He didn't want anyone to see him for who he was. Which was just fine by me because I was his walking billboard. I was the reflection of him. There was nothing he could say that would fix the situation or make him look any differently than what he was."

"So where are we today?" Minister Alexander took a deep breath. "I am here in your presence, that is obvious. And my husband is here with you too. In fact, you met him just a few minutes ago. When I put my business out in the streets and chose life, God stepped in with a quickness. I went to work the next day with a spring in my step and for the first time, my coworkers didn't tease me. Their imaginations were arrested with my reality. My supervisor, I thank God for her, shared with me her past and how much we had in common. She put me in place with contacts that were able to provide immediate housing to me. However, I had to refuse her offer. I went back to my home and never left. I had no reason to. It was mine. I continued to cook and clean as normal. Of course, my husband was suspect of my cooking. Nevertheless, I began to live life with a new purpose and mission. What was once in the dark, had now come to light."

"Oh, yeah. I didn't mean to leave you all hanging when I said that you already met my husband. Come here, sweetheart."

Jaynie looked over as Minister Roberts came back to the podium. Who would have known?

"Yes, family. Minister Roberts, our leader for Brothers Helping Brothers is in fact my husband. We have different last names because when I came back to the Lord I also went back to my maiden name. Why you ask? At that time, my husband was not loving me as his wife. In the bible, it says in Ephesians, "Husbands love you wives…. And wives, submit to your husbands." "Now I know there has been confusion about what submission is. Let me tell you what it is not. Submission does not require abuse, whether it is verbal, physical, sexual, financial, or emotional. In our time apart, my husband has grown in his relationship with the Lord and has finally come to himself. We will become one again on April 17. He now understands who my Daddy is and that I am a gift from God that has been given to him. I must be handled with care because I am His prized possession. In fact, we are all God's prized possessions. Women, again I say to you, you are fearfully and wonderfully made. Men, God has given you the charge to take care of your wives, your families, and your communities with the same love and reverence that you have for Him. It is important that you each refresh your relationship with the Lord and line up with the destiny and plans that he has had for you since the beginning of time."

That was it. Listening to Minister Alexander was all that Jaynie needed to make the decision to leave James. She knew that she wasn't strong enough to stay in her home, as Minister Alexander, however, she had to choose life. So she left. The four years that they were apart were times that were very difficult. Although James was very angry when she decided to leave, he refused to beg her to stay.

"So you think that you can make it on your own? There is going to be a time when you will come crawling back to me because I am the best thing you ever had." When Jaynie left, she only took what was necessary; her son, her clothes, her bank book, and her bible. James refused to give her the car that was a supposed birthday gift. He didn't give her any furniture whatsoever. Yet, he gave her the one thing that she desired. He gave her peace.

The day she walked into her destiny was also the last time that she saw James. After joining Women of Destiny and meeting with Minister Alexander during their intake interview, Jaynie was given temporary housing. Minister Alexander made it very clear. "If you have the desire to stay living in hell, then I cannot stop you. However, it is my responsibility to make sure that Lance does not take residency with you. Therefore, I will take him." Jaynie was taken aback but never expressed it. She did not want to lose her son or cause any more confusion in his life. They moved into their furnished one bedroom apartment the next day. During the week, she attended group meetings at the church. Each meeting required that the women complete homework assignments that helped to tear down the strongholds that were preventing them from recognizing that they were as daughters of the most high God. Although Jaynie hadn't experienced physical abuse until she was much older in life, she did however, discover that her childhood was filled with many instances of pain, hurt, and unresolved anger. Her childhood made it very easy for her to remain in unhealthy relationships.

The years went by and Jaynie's faith continued to grow. She began to remove all the baggage in her life by confronting it head on.

"Listen ladies. I understand that you are hurting," Minister Alexander spoke. "I understand that your husband, boyfriend, or lover has beaten some of you nearly to death. I've been there. However, I am not about to let you continue to play the victim role. The bottom line is this. We are going to share our pain this one and last time and then we are going to let it go. Then, I am going to break you down."

"What do you mean by that?" Each woman winced at those words.

"Don't you all realize that your life it just a symptom, a reflection of how you feel? It is not the root. Think about it this way. When you are sick, you may sneeze, cough, and have temperature. You may take cold medicine but that only masks the problem for a while. Some of you may shop till you drop, drink alcohol or take drugs as a pain reliever, or eat yourself to slow death as a way to self-medicate. Nevertheless, you still have not addressed the root of your illness.

Yet, when you begin to peel back the layers of your life and uncover the essence of your pain, you find out that it could be a whack immune system or mental fatigue. When you treat the specifics, it alters your whole body. The same is for you all here in this class. Before you can ever have a relationship with anyone, you much first have a relationship is the Lord. He is your source."

Minister Alexander went to the marker board and drew a giant L. "Love. Before you can extend your hands to those that are around you, you must first extend your hands to the Lord. Unfortunately, we tend not to think about Him, as we should, especially when we are feeling hurt, isolated, or depressed. We wonder if God is there at all when we are getting our faces bashed in. And if He is there, why hasn't He stepped in to make it stop. Yes ladies, your relationship with the Lord must be examined and given top priority in life. Then you will begin your journey in uncovering your destiny. When you come to the end of you, then God can take over."

God began to take over Jaynie's life with a fierceness. Jaynie worshipped the Lord in everything that she did, with everything that she had. There were no regrets because her life with James was the catalyst to bring her back to her rightful place with the Lord.

However, there was a part of her that still wondered where James was in his life away from her. Although she did not verbalize it, Jaynie felt somewhat sad that James allowed her to leave without begging her to stay. How could he fight her without a thought, yet, never fight for her.

"God, I need to let that go. If it was meant for us to stay together, you would have allowed it." Yet, Kool Moe Dee's old school rap tune, *How you Like Me Now?* continued to resonate in her spirit. Although Jaynie grew in her faith, she was still lonely. Lance was doing well in school but she always wondered if things could have been different. If she only knew then, what she knew now.

God has a way of giving us the desires of our heart because a few weeks later, Jaynie ran into James at the Worship and Praise Conference at the Atlanta Civic Center. To say that she was surprised would have been an understatement. She was flabbergasted. James and God just did not fit together. *Lord, you are able to do all things. If you were able to change my mind, then I know you are able to change his.*

Expecting the unexpected, Jaynie decided to meet up with James for a cup of coffee at Starbucks the next day. Through small talk, she learned that James had brought his mom to the conference that day. She shared the fact that Lance was continuing to flourish in his schoolwork and was now a part of the football team. Jaynie complimented Jaynie on how beautiful she was, while Jaynie said that he still was as handsome as ever. Their small talk continued, yet, it never developed into deep conversation.

"Jaynie, you seem different. I can't put my finger on it."

"I am different. I had to let a lot of things go. I had to let go of my past."

"How were you able to do that? Were you able to let go of me? You took my son and walked out of my life without even looking back."

"What are you talking about? James, we were living all wrong. Besides the fact that we were never married, we would also fight."

"I know. I know. But it was nothing. I still had your back."

"How can you say that it was nothing? Do you remember anything?"

"Of course I remember. It's just that we were both young and didn't know any better. I've changed and it's apparent that you have too."

"I know. I'm as shocked as ever. I never would have thought that the day would come when we would sit down and actually talk again."

Jaynie needed to pinch herself. "Am I dreaming, Lord?"

"Look, James. I really must go. I have several more errands to run. It was nice seeing you again."

"Jaynie, wait. Umm, do you think that we might be able to get together again? You know, for a cup of coffee or maybe to talk."

"I don't know. It's still too soon."

"Well, I thought you said that you had to let a lot of things go. You never answered my question. Did you let me go?" James looked at Jaynie with expectancy in his eyes.

"James, I don't know what to say. Look, I have to go. I'll talk to you later."

"Can I call you sometimes? Maybe I can speak to Lance."

"That would be fine. Here is my number." Jaynie gave her telephone number and left Starbucks.

"Lord, I am definitely going to need your help on this one. "

From that moment on, James called Jaynie every day. Always starting his conversation with small talk, he would always end it the same way. *Have you let me go?* Jaynie continued to go to group meetings but never shared the fact that she had spoken to James. It seemed as if she was now fraternizing with the enemy.

"Ladies, there will come a time when we all have to come face to face with our fears. Fear is False Evidence Appearing Real. Just remember that. I am not saying that you should search out your abuser, but just know that when the time comes, remember that the Lord is there with you. Just as he has been in the past. I also know that you may be feeling conflicting emotions about the one who has hurt you. This is a critical time in your life. You still love him yet you are afraid of him."

Jaynie felt heat rise through her shirt. "Minister Alexander cannot possibly know," she thought to herself. "How much longer is this class?"

"Jaynie, can I talk to you before you leave?"

"Why sure."

"Jaynie, I know that this may not be the best time for you but I really need your help. I have watched you grow over the past few years. When I met you, you had just left James. You were scared, alone, and unsure of yourself. Over the past few years, you have grown into a woman of god who speaks with wisdom. You have ministered to many of the sisters that have come through our group. While many have graduated, you have chosen to stay on and continue to serve. I am very pleased with your loyalty."

"Why thank you, Minister Alexander. I am truly honored to hear this."

"Jaynie, I am going to ask you to help run several of our upcoming classes. Don't worry. It will not be difficult. You are pretty much going to do the same thing that you do now. I'll walk you through everything."

Jaynie was mixed with emotion. Why had she been chosen for such a monumental task, especially at a time like this?

"Look, Jaynie. Just pray on it and let me know what you think. Let us pray before we leave."

"Dear Heavenly Father, I ask that you cover each and every woman that has come through our doors. Leaving their past was a difficult thing for them to do. However, taking this step towards you can be the hardest thing that they will ever do. Lord, many of these women have been abused in ways that we can only imagine; however, you Lord know the depths of their pain and hurt. Lord please step in and allow your Holy Spirit to move mightily inside each and everyone of them. Give them the peace and joy that only you can give. We need you Lord to move in quickly. Lord, I ask that you please guide Jaynie in her decision to move into a leadership role for our group. Although I know that she will lift up your kingdom to those who are brokenhearted, I also know that you are the one who sets the appointed time. Lord, I thank you and give you all the praise, honor, and glory. In Jesus Christ's name we pray, Amen."

At that moment, Jaynie knew that her decision would be yes. Although it had been painful to uncover her true identity, Jaynie realized that in order for her to let go of her past, she needed to first understand it. Not excusing James' abusive nature, Jaynie realized that her childhood disappointments produced a girl who had low self-esteem, feared rejection, and would do anything for love. James wasn't the first person to hurt Jaynie: it's just that his scars were visible.

"Minister Alexander, I would be honored to serve under you leadership. However, I need to tell you something."

"What is it?"

"James has been contacting me. We met for coffee the other day and talked for a long time. In fact, I was surprised because I wasn't as afraid as I thought I would be."

"That's because you know that the Lord is with you." Minister Alexander looked at Jaynie. "Is there something else on your mind?"

"Well, James kept asking me if I let him go. I never answered him."

"Why not?"

"I don't know. No matter how far I have come in my faith, there is a part of me that still wishes things would have worked out between us. It wasn't like we fought all the time."

"Jaynie, you know like I know. One time is enough. That's all that it takes."

"I know. But you stayed."

"Yes, I did stay. There is a part of me that wonders if my staying is the right example for you women. As much as I remind you all to have a plan, I did the total opposite. Yes, I thank God that he was able to move in my life and touch my husband's heart, but Jaynie, that doesn't always happen."

"Look," Minister Alexander continued, "the same way that I ask you to pray about your decision to move up to group facilitator, I also ask that you pray about your relationship with James. Only God can show you what to do."

Kayla and Sharee arrived at the Soul at 7:45 am.

"Isn't God good?" Kayla spoke

"Who are you telling." Sharee answered. "Girl, I still cannot believe that this is a shelter. It looks like a mansion."

"I know. When I drove through the area last summer, I could not stop driving by this house. Although it was out of my league, I kept saying, "Lord, if only I had this. I could provide housing to so many women." Kayla took a deep breath. "I remember when I first thought about leaving Tyson. Up until that moment, I had not even entertained the idea of being out of his sight. Not because I loved him so much, but because he made sure that I accounted for my every moment away from me. We were going through our silent periods and I was enjoying it as hell. By that time, I hated to even hear his voice."

"Hmmph, I can imagine."

"Anyway, I was browsing through one of my magazines and there it was. A six-bedroom house sitting on a basement. Shoot, my mind started turning. I couldn't sleep at night. So one night, I got down on my knees and said, "Lord, if you can take my situation and turn it into good, I promise that you will get all the glory.""

"I guess God took you up on your promise." Sharee conceded.

"He sure did. I walked into the sales office and told the saleslady my story. At first she was kind of concerned about the situation, you know, a lot of people really don't want to talk about domestic violence."

"Well, then, what changed her mind?" Sharee asked.

"The Lord, of course. All she could say was that the Lord had laid it on her heart to help me get that house. And it is perfect."

"I can see that." Sharee answered as she walked through the foyer. It was definitely perfect.

"I know. That's why I call it The Soul. That's why I named my business Soul Simplicities. As auspicious as this house is, it represents the simplicities of life. Girl, it's all about having space. There's room for everyone to grow." Kayla thought, "When I was with Tyson, my life only revolved around him. I was never able to think outside the box, to dream."

"Girl, I ain't dreamed in a long time."

"Neither had I. But I do know what it's like to not have a dream, to exist without a purpose. I never thought about having possibilities. In fact, many women who leave violent situations are searching for one thing- freedom. Going into a shelter isn't always the best solution for them. You can feel just as imprisoned as when you were in the abusive relationship."

"I hear you. I have heard that it can be very difficult for many women to move into a shelter."

"Absolutely. There are many women who are fleeing from their homes with just the clothes on their back. If they have children, they then have to contend with the fact that their children will have left everything behind, as well. Regardless of how jacked up our lives are, unfortunately our pride can get in the way and make us feel as if we are taking a step backwards. Many times, there are women who are overqualified and cannot get assistance. Therefore, they go back home and wait out their death sentence."

"I hear you. There aren't enough resources available to women at this critical time in their life."

"I wanted to provide a safe haven to these women so that they will be less apt to go back," Kayla confessed. "During the time that they are here at the Soul, they can take care of their souls. I have several counselors on staff that can provide support and resources to them. My cousin is going to handle all of the maintenance and security. And of course, I am living here too."

"That's what I don't understand. Why are you going to live here? Isn't it dangerous to do such a thing?"

"Of course, anything this emotional can be risky. However, I am willing to go through whatever it is so that I can help those around me. Believe me, God is all up in the midst."

Sharee and Kayla continued walking through the house.

"By my living here, it will be like having my own family over during the holidays. When I was with Tyson, I never experienced that. He just did not like my family. However, what I have come to realize is that he never wanted anyone to be privy to what was going on behind closed doors. He wanted us to stay isolated. My mistake was in allowing that to happen."

"Why did you allow it to happen? Girl, we have known each other for so long and you even separated from me. There were times when I was angry because it seemed like you were cool with all of that."

"I don't know," Kayla admitted. "When I think about it, in the beginning of our relationship, I was cool with it. We were getting to know one another and I wanted to spend as much time with him as possible. He was my life. Or at least I thought he was."

"So when did things start to change?"

"After a while, I felt secure enough in our relationship and wanted us to spend time with not just you, but with my family, also. But Tyson would always start to trip. He would play with my emotions and say that we were the family now. Including others into our life will be a distraction from taking care of home," Kayla admitted. "When I would spend time with others, it was always a problem. Either he wouldn't speak to me when I came home or he would drill me about all the things that I did. It was just easier not to make waves. I wanted to see you all but I also wanted to make him happy too."

Although Sharee felt rejected, she understood where Kayla was coming from. There were times when she accommodated Robert to keep the peace in the house.

As the two women continued on through the Soul, they explored the various bedrooms. Each room, decorated with muted colors of yellows, greens, and beiges, had a queen sized bed, a dresser, and a full-length mirror. There was nothing else.

"Wow, I would have expected more to be in the bedrooms. Why are they so empty?" Sharee questioned.

"Empty? I don't think that they are empty. They have a queen-sized bed so that each woman can spread out when she sleeps. I remember when I was with Tyson. I stayed on my side of the bed, you know, whichever side he didn't want. Even after I separated from him, I still slept in the same space on the right side of the bed. But after a lot of soul searching, I realized that I like to sleep on the left side, the right side, and in the middle. It just depends on how I am feeling at the time."

"I never thought of it that way."

"It's those simple things that we never think about that was the most important to me when I was finally free from him. When you are in abusive relationship, you are constantly thinking. Did I do this the right way? Did I do that the right way? Is he going to be angry tonight? Will we fight? It's a constant battle. And you know what I have learned. It's a battle that you can never win."

"Why do you say that?" Sharee curiously asked.

"I say that because it's true. Right before I left Tyson, I told him that I was tired of jumping through hoops trying to please him. I felt like it was a losing battle because nothing I had done was ever correct. And do you know what he said?"

"No, what?"

"He said that his job was to keep me on my toes. He was doing it for my benefit. He needed to teach me how to think in all situations. He said he was doing me a favor."

"Did you believe him?"

"Of course, I didn't believe him but by this time, I had given up. I stopped trying to over think him and just stopped thinking."

Kayla began to reflect on her choices. "Hmm. I still think that this room has just enough. Do you see that dresser and mirror over there?

"Yes, I do" Sharee answered.

"Well, I chose just these two pieces for one reason. I chose the dresser because the women who come here will need a new wardrobe. More than likely, they will have left all that they had behind to escape. They are going to need clothes. Not just any clothes, but clothes that will make them proud. It took me a long time to buy clothes just for me."

"What do you mean?"

"When I dressed, I dressed for Tyson. My clothes had to look a certain way, nothing too revealing. I didn't want to bring attention to myself in anyway. God forbid, another man glanced my way. I must have provoked him. But through the grace of God, I learned to like me again. I learned to see myself with new eyes, God's eyes. It wasn't easy but I thank God."

"I guess that's why you chose the mirror."

"See, now you are beginning to understand. I chose a full-length mirror because it is the one thing that I hated with a passion. It showed all of me, from top to bottom. The bruises, the scars, the tear stained eyes. My disheveled hair, my unkempt clothes, my broken spirit. But girl now, I can walk in front of a mirror and actually like what I see. It wasn't easy but I thank God."

Kayla walked to the mirror and began to primp and pose.

"That's when I'll know that a woman is ready to move on into life. When she can look in a mirror and say, "Don't I look good," then I will know that she will not lose herself ever again. She will carry herself in a different way and accept nothing less than what she deserves. Nothing less than what God has planned for her because she will know who she is and whose she is. God is so good!"

"I never thought of it that way."

"Exactly. Because God's thoughts are not our thoughts. His thoughts of us are beautiful. Come on. Let me show you the rooms for the children."

The peace and tranquility for the women was replaced with the excitement and exuberance for children.

"I cannot wait until I hear the laughter from my babies. Children are wonderful." Kayla spoke into the air.

"Yes, they are. I think about my nieces and nephews and how they make me laugh." Sharee agreed.

"I know. Although I don't have children, I know a few things about them. They are resilient and observant. Many times, we think that our children are unaware of everything that goes on behind closed doors. Hopefully, it is behind closed doors because children do not need to see, hear, or get caught up in their parent's hell."

Sharee silently thanked God that she never had any children because they would be devastated if she and Robert ever split up.

"This room right here is their entertainment center. I have the TV, flat screen of course, Playstation 3 and X Box. I also have a library set up with the latest magazines, books, and videos. I didn't forget to fill it up with the latest movies. I have a couple of walkmans for the times when they may want to be alone. There may be some teenagers coming through here. I have two computers set up in that corner for homework assignments and browsing the internet. I think that I just about covered everything."

"Yes, you have. The sofa and recliners fit in just perfectly. But what about their bedrooms."

"At first, I was going to let them share a room with their mother but it will depend on the circumstances and her condition. That is why I have two rooms set up with bunk beds. If their mother wants them with her, then I have some cots stored up in my basement."

"So where are you going to sleep?" Sharee asked.

"My bedroom in on the main floor. Come on. Let me show it to you."

Kayla and Sharee walked back downstairs through the living room and down the hallway. She opened the door to her bedroom.

"Whoa, now. Will you look at this?" Sharee spoke excitedly.

Kayla stood back with a smile on her face. "What do you think?"

"Wow, it is gorgeous." In the center of her bedroom was a king-sized mahogany sleigh bed that seemed to sit ten feet off the ground.

"Do you think that it is high enough," Kayla asked. "I wanted something that was as high up as possible. I have to admit, it was some getting used to. There's my footstool over there. Do you want to give it a try?"

Sharee walked over to the footstool and hoisted herself up. She laid down on the bed and stared up at the ceiling. Right above her head, she thought she saw heaven. Literally.

"Kayla, baby, is that the sky?"

"Yes, it is. I had someone come in and paint it for me. I also had them put in that skylight. The way this house is built, there aren't any rooms overhead. That's why it could be done. So now, when I wake up in the morning, God's light shines all over me. When I lay my head down at night," Kayla shut off the lights and closed the blinds to her room, "I can see the stars in heaven's night sky."

Sharee's eyes adjusted to the darkness of the room. And there she saw it. Stars filled the sky. Tears filled her eyes. "I remember when I was a young girl. I used to look up to the stars in the sky and wonder in amazement. How did they get there? How far away were they? Then I would make a wish."

"What did you wish for?" Kayla asked

"I don't know. It wasn't for a man. I guess it was for happy times. I always wanted happy times" Sharee admitted.

"I did too." Kayla confirmed, "I would dream about how I wanted my life to be when I grew up. My life. My husband. My job. My life didn't turn out as I expected."

"Neither did mine."

The women both stayed in silence for a while.

"Sharee," Kayla asked, "when did we stop dreaming?"

"I don't know, girl. I don't know."

Kayla walked over to a set of doors to the left.

"I don't know when I stopped dreaming but I do know when I started to dream again."

She opened the doors and walked in.

Sharee tried to adjust to the lighting of the still darkened room and slowly climbed off the bed to following the softly dimmed light before her.

"Here it is," Kayla spoke after Sharee had entered the room.

"This is where I started dreaming again," Kayla spoke.

Inside the room, there was a small chaise lounge, decorated in royal purple and gold. To the right side, there was a small fountain with cascading water flowing from its spout. To the left of the sofa, there sat a small altar, covered with candles. A bible lay on the altar opened to Psalm 139.

"This is my prayer room. I call it my Dream Machine. It's the first place I come to in the morning and the last place I come to in the evening. When I am sad, I come in here and when I am overjoyed, I come in here. There is a feeling of peace as soon as you enter."

Sharee felt it, too. "Hmmph, Kayla. This is too much. You have seemed to capture everything that I want as a woman. And it's all so simple, yet so extraordinary."

"It's all about simplicity. God doesn't ask any more of us. That's why we are called Soul's Simplicities. Or what I really like, The Soul. Women may come in here feeling weary, frightened, and alone, but I guarantee you that when they leave they will feel full of life, strengthened, and closer to the Lord," Kayla affirmed.

"Now, that's what I'm talking about. Hmmph, I need to be in a place like this but I'm not in an abusive situation like the women you are going to serve. Robert isn't hitting all up on me," Sharee spoke with confidence.

"Sharee, you cannot possibly believe that it's just about physical abuse. No, baby, abuse is abuse. Whether it's physical, emotional, financial, or mental. It's all the same. If it's hurting you, it's abusive. If it's causing you to lose you, then its abusive. If it's pulling you away from your relationship with the Lord, it is abusive. No matter what form it's in, it is still wrong. This place is not just for the physically abused, it's for those who have given up on living life to the fullest, those who have stopped dreaming."

The two women stood silently in the prayer room.

"Sharee, have you stopped dreaming?" Kayla asked softly.

Sharee turned around, walked out of the prayer room, and returned to the living room without uttering a sound.

"Yes, Kayla, I have stopped dreaming."

Jennifer and Officer Conners arrived late in the evening. After securing several of Jennifer's belongings, they made the journey to the Soul in absolute silence.

"You know you're doing the right thing, don't you" Officer Conners spoke

"Um-hm."

"I promise you that things are going to turn around for you."

"Um-hm."

"If you need me, please know that you can call anytime. Here's my card."

"Uh-hm" Jennifer reached out and grabbed the business card.

Silence loomed in the air.

"It's not your fault" Officer Conners tried to reassure Jennifer.

Officer Conners waited for a response but never got one.

Driving down the pathway to the house, Officer Conners let out a soft whistle. "Will you look at this place? Now, Kayla told me that this place was out the box, but this is too ridiculous. What kind of shelter is this?"

"It doesn't look like a shelter to me" Jennifer agreed. "What's up with all of this?"

"Your guess is as good as mine. I've known Kayla for many years and have seen her go through just about anything and everything. How she has managed to survive is beyond me. But she has and I am sure that you two will get along."

"You think so, hmmph. Why is that?" Jennifer asked.

"Due to the simple fact that you are here with me in this car. I cannot even count the number of times when I have offered help to a hurting woman and she refused. It gets to be very discouraging. Yet, tonight you decided to trust me without hesitation. Hope is definitely alive."

"I wouldn't say all of that. I chose to come with you because I do not have any other place to go to. I can't go home. I don't want to go to a shelter. And I haven't spoken to my family in years. You could say that I had no choice."

"We always have a choice. You could have very well told me to leave you alone. But you didn't. Why?"

"As much as I want to run, I realize that you were being very truthful to me when you shared your story about your best friend. You didn't have to be so real with me. Who am I? You didn't even know me."

"I didn't need to know you to be honest with you." Officer Conners spoke. "All I needed to do was to tell the truth. Losing Lisa was the worse thing in the world but I made her a promise; that I would help any woman that needed help."

"That's a huge cross to bear."

"I know it is. But I thank God that I am not bearing it alone. I have all the help that I need."

"What do you mean by that?"

"I have the help of Jesus Christ. He is definitely my rock." Officer Conners looked up to the sky.

"Hmmph. If you say so. I've never met him."

"I can tell but that's OK. He's met you and that's all that you need."

"What do you mean by that?" Jennifer asked quizzically.

"Just what I said. There is going to be a time when you two will formally introduce yourselves but for now, just get to know you. You said that I didn't know you well enough to help you. Well let me ask you this. Do you know yourself well enough to know you?"

"See, now you are starting to talk all deep and everything. Of course I know myself. I know what I like and what I don't like."

"Do you think that's enough? To simplify your existence to what you like and don't like."

"It's gotten me this far."

"Yes, it has. But has that been with or without problems?"

Jennifer mulled over Officer Conner's question. She made many decisions based upon her emotions. When she left her parent's home, she realized that it was because she didn't like how her father abused her mom. Yet, she stayed with Jason even though she did not like the fact that he was abusive. Her existence was the mirror image of her mother's existence.

"I get it, Officer Conners."

"Uh-hm. I know you do." Officer Conners parked the car in front of the Soul and both women exited the vehicle.

"Jennifer?"

"Yes?"

"You don't have to keep calling me Officer Conners. My friend's call me Celeste."

"I get it, Officer… I mean Celeste."

Within a few seconds, the front door opened and there stood Kayla.

"Welcome, welcome, welcome to the Soul. Mi casa es tu casa."

"Oh, Jennifer, I forgot to tell you" Officer Conners spoke. "Kayla here is a self-proclaimed Latina. She seems to feel that studying Spanish on an audiotape is enough for her to cross over to the other side."

"Very funny, Celeste. Come here, girl, and give me a hug."

Celeste gave her best friend a tight squeeze. "Girl, this place is amazing."

"I know. It had to be. Especially for the amazing women who are going to cross its threshold. Like you, sweetie." Kayla looked over at Jennifer with a gleam in her eyes. "I see greatness in you."

Shocked with her revelation, Jennifer put her head down. "Greatness? I only see a black eye and busted lip."

"That's only the surface, baby. It goes much deeper than that. Come in. Come in."

The women entered the foyer.

"Let me have your coats." Kayla took Celeste's jacket and Jennifer's sweater and placed them in the closet.

"Celeste, if you will excuse me, I am going to take Jennifer to her room."

Jennifer looked at Celeste for confirmation. "Who is this woman and why am I supposed to trust her?" she thought.

Celeste nodded her head and winked her eye. "You go, girl," she whispered.

Kayla led Jennifer upstairs to her new bedroom and Celeste made her way through the house into the living area.

"You go, girl." Celeste whispered to herself. Lisa loved to affirm her sister-girls whenever they did something spectacular. Martin was Lisa's favorite television show. Lisa loved to see Gina's face light up when he spoke these words to her. He was telling her that he had her back in whatever she decided to do. He would be there whenever she came back home.

"You are tripping. How in the world can you read all of that in three little words," Celeste would ask Lisa.

"How can I not. Do you realize how special it is to hear someone; whether it is your parents or your man, tell you they got your back? They are confident in your skills and will always be there for you. It's sort of like saying "You do you."

Only until after Lisa's death did Celeste understand the impact of those three words. Lisa lived her life waiting for Ryan to affirm her but unfortunately it never happened. Nevertheless, Lisa made sure that she affirmed those closest to her. "You go, girl" was like her stamp of approval and seemed to remove all limitations from the situation.

Now Celeste found herself using the same words for Kayla. The limitations had been taken off and Kayla's dream had actually manifested. Standing in the living area was truth to it. Browsing through the books on the built-in bookcase, Celeste's attention was drawn to one in particular. *The Power of Forgiveness*.

Forgiveness. Is it possible to forgive someone for abusing you? Is it possible to forgive yourself for allowing the abuse? Celeste struggled with these two questions.

"Hmmph, I can forgive but I will be damned if I ever forget." Celeste spoke out loud.

"I hear you. I feel the same way." A voice spoke in the background.

Celeste turned around and there stood Sharee.

"Sharee? Is that you?"

"In the flesh, my dear. All of this flesh." Sharee waved her arms across her body.

"Girl, you better get over here and give me a hug. Kayla didn't tell me you were going to be here."

"I wasn't supposed to be," Sharee admitted. "But I thank God that I am now. Did you get a chance to look at this place? It is absolutely amazing."

"That's what I was just thinking to myself. How was Kayla able to pull this off?"

"I don't know. But what I do know is that Kayla has the hand of God on her shoulder."

"Yes she does." Celeste responded. "So what brings you here. How's Robert doing? I hadn't seen you all in years."

"Robert is doing fine. I'm just here to help my girl out."

"That's what I mean. I never expected you to be involved in this type of arrangement. You and Robert can't possibly have problems like this."

Sharee looked at Celeste. "How can you say such a thing?"

"I don't mean no harm at all. It's just that you two seem like the perfect couple. Robert is handsome, hardworking, and loves you so much. And you are beautiful, intelligent, and loyal to the fullest. What could possibly go wrong?"

"You shouldn't ever assume, Celeste. You know that."

"I know. So, I tell you what, enlighten me on my assumptions."

"Well the truth of the matter is that Robert and I seemed to be very happy. I loved him just as much as he loved me." Sharee took a deep breath.

"So what's the problem and why are you speaking in past tense."

"Celeste, unfortunately, our love was all a lie. You see, Robert doesn't just love me. He loves…"

"Come on now, don't tell me that Robert is out there fooling around on you. What is it about a man that makes him want to be doggish? One woman ain't enough."

"Celeste, can you let me finish. Robert has cheated on me in the past but I was able to work through it. I stepped up my game. But this time, I have to throw in the towel because there is no way that I can compete."

"Compete with what. You're just as beautiful as the next woman."

"Why thank you but I am not competing against a woman. I am competing against…"

It quickly registered in Celeste's mind.

"A man", both women chimed in at the same time.

"Jennifer, please make yourself comfortable. Here is your room."

Jennifer looked around her bedroom at the sparseness. "Why thank you very much. I appreciate it."

"Don't worry about it. There are a few items in the closet that I hope will fit you. We seem to be about the same size. When I made up the bedrooms here in the house, I made sure that I was able to have an ample amount of clothing available to both the women and their children. "

"Wow, you seemed not to leave out any details."

"I couldn't. I've been there. I had to leave in the blink of the eye and it wasn't easy. Yet I prayed to God, that if there was ever another woman in need, please grant me the ability to provide for her until she is able to get on her feet."

Jennifer went to the closet to peruse the items that were in there. "There are so many clothes here. All with the tags on them. Please tell me that you did not spend all of your money."

"No, I didn't spend all of my money. I spent just enough. When I left Tyson, no let me change that, when I ran away from Tyson, I ran away from everything. It took a lot for me to leave him because my life totally revolved around him. It was to the point where I decided everything for me, down to the clothing that I wore. He reminded me every day that he was the one who made me who I was. So when I got up enough courage to leave him, I refused to take a stitch of anything that he bought me." Kayla began to walk around the room. "I literally went from rags to riches. It wasn't easy either. I learned the importance of thrift stores and dollar stores because that was all that I could afford. Thank God, I was still able to work. I had a decent salary but now my living conditions had changed dramatically."

"I hear you. Unfortunately, I am between jobs so my income is limited… to zip."

"That's why your time here is going to be special. This is the time when you can focus on who you are and what you plan to do with the rest of your life. It is your life, don't forget that. And God has had a plan for you since the beginning of time."

"I'm not so sure about that." Jennifer sadly admitted.

"It's OK if you feel that way at this moment. Right now you are in a difficult situation. However, in time you will see how this unfortunate situation can be used for good. I promise you that."

"How can you make a promise of that magnitude. Right now, I am homeless, broke, and alone."

"You were homeless. Remember, mi casa es tu casa. You were broken but we all need to be broken at one time or another so that God can put us back together in his way. And alone. You were alone but I am here and so is Celeste. But the only person who can restore you is our God."

"What's up with God. Everywhere I turn, someone is speaking about Him. He doesn't care about me. If he did, I wouldn't be in this situation. Look at me. I am a mess."

Jennifer ran to the mirror and looked at her face. It was still puffy and swollen from Jason's punches.

"Those scars will heal in time. What I'm talking about are the scars that are on the inside of you. You've been hurting for a long time, haven't you?"

"Yes, but…."

"Don't worry about it." Kayla put her index finger to her lips. "You don't have to explain anything to me right now. It has been a long day. Why don't you go in the bathroom and take a relaxing bath. There is still some time before we have lunch. I've left some fresh towels in the bathroom, along with, some wonderful bubble baths. There are so many varieties available because I couldn't just choose one. I love them all. Of course, I have my favorite but you choose your own."

Kayla turned around to walk out of the bedroom. "Jennifer, sweetie, I am going to promise you this one thing. I promise that when you are ready, you will love yourself just as God loves you. And sweetie, he loves you so much."

Having made her proclamation, Kayla walked out of the bedroom and down the stairs to join Celeste once again.

"Please, please pick up the phone."

Jaynie had called Minister Alexander on a whim. She was the only one who could understand. How had things turned out so wrong between Jaynie and James? Their love was supposed to conquer all, that's what the bible said. Minister Alexander and her husband were proof of this.

"Hello."

"Uh, hello. Minister Alexander. It's Jaynie."

"Hey Jaynie how are you. Why do you insist on calling me Minister Alexander? We aren't at church. It's Kim."

"I know. I know. Uh, I need to speak with you. It's very important."

"Jaynie, what's the matter. Something's wrong."

"I... uh, I need help."

"Jaynie, where are you. I am on my way."

Jaynie drove around in circles after dropping Lance off at his best friend's house. Not wanting to get out of the car, she briefly explained the situation to Tony's mother. Lance would be very upset, but if possible, could she lighten his mood. Thank God for the Nichols. If anyone could do it, it was him or her. Sam and Jessica Nichols were the happiest couple Jaynie had ever met. They always included Lance in on their family outings and celebrations. Lance and Tony were best friends since fourth grade.

"Take all the time that you need, Jaynie. You know that Lance is like our second son."

Arrangements were made that Lance would stay with them until Jaynie found other living arrangements. Thank God she had a plan.

"God, how can you let this happen? You told me to go back."

Jaynie was angry that things had to end like this. Up until that fateful moment, she and James rarely argued. He never raised his hands to her or expressed the need to. Although they argued, it was never enough for Jaynie to feel afraid like before.

Jaynie had been in the grips of fear for many years when she and James were first together. Their fighting was not on a consistent basis as Minister Alexander stated, yet the times when they fought, it was pretty bad. James would usually throw a tantrum when he did not get his way or give Jaynie the silent treatment. He might have thrown a remote across the room and busted a hole in the wall but it was never in Jaynie's direction. He may have called Jaynie lazy or stupid but he never disrespected her by calling her a bitch.

I cannot believe you are actually rationalizing his behavior. You know better. Abuse is abuse. It's all the same.

Jaynie knew this to be true however, she couldn't help it. She knew all the signs. As a domestic violence counselor, she reiterated the signs of abuse to victims each week. However, she still could not help excusing his behavior.

Knock. Knock. Knock. Minister Alexander was knocking on Jaynie's car window in the Target parking lot. Jaynie was startled.

"Oh, Minister Alexander, it's you. You scared me."

"Jaynie, baby, open the door so that we can talk. Do you want to stay here or should we go somewhere else."

"I think it will be safe here. Come on in."

Minister Alexander walked around the car and got in on the passenger side.

"Jaynie, what happened?"

Jaynie tried to speak but immediately choked up.

"Take your time, sweetie."

"I had to leave James."

"Why. Did he hit you?"

"No, he didn't hit me. I didn't give him enough time to. Instead, I hit him".

"Why did you hit him?"

"I couldn't help it. He was yelling and screaming at me and I was afraid. I haven't been afraid in years." Jaynie began to cry.

"I understand. How about if you start from the beginning and tell me exactly what happened."

Jaynie took a deep breath. "I couldn't do it anymore. I couldn't live a lie any longer."

"What do you mean?"

"I know that I told you that I was happy with James. Our relationship seemed different than before. We weren't fighting anymore. I was a different person and so was he, at least I thought he was."

"You did tell me that. I remember."

"But I wasn't totally honest with you or myself. James didn't raise his hands to me but he still hurt me in subtle ways. He was still angry because I left him the first time."

"That's understandable" Minister Alexander confirmed, "but I thought you two had worked through that situation. Did you try counseling?"

"I never thought about counseling. I thought my coming to Women of Destiny was enough."

"It was enough for you and I have seen a tremendous difference in your demeanor and attitude. However, James needed to go to counseling as well, individually and together as a couple."

"You're right," Jaynie agreed. "However, in the past few months I have started questioning our relationship. We were back together for two years yet James refused to marry me. I know that living together was all wrong, but I felt that we would one day make it right. Unfortunately, that never happened."

"That happens to a lot of couples."

"I know. So each week, as I counseled other women, I realized that I wasn't being truthful. I felt convicted each day and needed to make things right. I tried speaking to James to tell him that it was wrong but he always said the same thing. We have been living like this for years and it has never been a problem before."

"OK. Keep going."

"He refused to move out so I began to make changes. I slowly started packing and setting a plan in place. I know from counseling that having a plan is important. I told James that I was leaving by the end of the month and he seemed to be OK with it. He didn't try to stop me."

"So then, what happened?"

"He didn't try to stop me, or at least I thought that. We weren't arguing and I tried to keep our daily schedule on track. The only difference is that I moved into the front bedroom and stopped sleeping with him. James tried to persuade me but I just couldn't do it anymore."

"How did James feel about you not sleeping together?"

"He was upset but he never pressured me. He thought that it was a temporary thing and I would come begging him for some attention but let me tell you, once I started on my mission to leave, all my desire left too. So, I packed up my things last night and told James that I would be leaving today."

"So I can assume that Lance was with you this morning."

"Yes, he was. Even though I did not have an apartment in place, I did place most of my things in storage. I spoke with my sister and she said that I could stay with her a while until I got myself together. Anyway, Lance and I were putting the last bags in the car and I went back inside to get my bible. James was there in the kitchen. I went to my room, gathered my bible and headed for the side door." Jaynie began to reflect on that moment in time.

"James was already standing there."

"I cannot believe that you are really going to leave," he said. "I told him that it was for the best and we would see how things would go later."

"He started yelling at me and getting in my face. I couldn't take it anymore. I asked him to let me leave but he refused. Then he started calling me every name in the book. He said that I thought I was better than him because I was in church. He said that going to church wouldn't change the fact that I was still a murderer. I never shared it with you that when James and I first got together years ago, I found out that I was pregnant. I couldn't keep the baby because our relationship wasn't stable. We were fighting real bad back then and James was drinking. I know it was wrong to have an abortion but I didn't know what else to do."

"Did James know that you were having one?"

"Yes, he did. In fact, he took me to the appointment. However, after it happened, he kept calling me a slut and a killer. I already felt guilty but then I felt dirty. I guess that's one of the reasons why I stayed with James so long. I felt as if I had no choice. I made my bed and needed to lie in it."

"Jaynie, you do know that God has forgiven you?"

"I know that but I had not forgiven myself. Not until I started coming to church. The closer I became to the Lord, the more freer I felt. God changed me. I stopped feeling guilty and ashamed and began to love myself. I realized that James' abuse was bad but abusing myself was even worse."

"When you offered me the counseling position, I felt the redemptive power of the Lord. I know that I wasn't worthy yet the Lord loved me enough to choose me for such a position. That's one of the reasons why I chose to give James a second chance. If the Lord was able to forgive me for my discretions, I could at least forgive James. Who am I to judge?"

"I understand."

"I don't know. I guess I was on an ego trip. I felt that I could change the world, you know. I guess that was all a joke, right."

"No it wasn't. You were trying to live your life as God expects us all to. Although I am always concerned about the women who are in abusive situations, I cannot help that. However, I realize my limitations. Every woman has to decide for themselves where they want to be. I only provide the tools to help them make the decision."

"I know. I have learned so much under your counsel. I can't help but think about your explanation of forgiveness. It took me a while to get it at first but now I truly understand. First, I need to ask god for forgiveness. Then I need to forgive myself. I need to forgive the person who has hurt me. Lastly, I have to be willing to put myself out there again."

"Yeah, that's the hard part. There aren't too many people who will put themselves out there to be hurt again. How does the saying go; Shame me once, shame on you. Shame me twice, shame on me."

"It was hard but I had to put myself out there again. I wasn't sure of how things were going to turn out between James and I but I do know that God told me to go back home to James. Does that make sense?"

"It makes a lot of sense. When I first met you, you were full of fear. You were afraid to make a mistake. You were afraid to make a move. You were afraid to live. Yet, over the next few months, you slowly began to come out of your shell. You stayed in the word and became a living example that God does give us a spirit of fear. You overcame so much."

"Yes. Hmph. I can even swim now. Lord knows, I was deathly afraid of that."

"I know. But the bottom line is that you overcame it. That's why I can understand you when you say that God sent you back to James. He needed you to face your biggest fear. James knew you before you were saved. He knew about your abortion. He knew about your guilt and shame."

"Yes, he did."

"James also knew the changes that had taken place in your life. When you left him the first time, you were supposed to fail but you didn't. When you met him at Starbucks, he needed to know if you let him go. Even though he waited for your response, he already knew your answer. You couldn't hide your glow. The light of the Lord was shining all through you."

"But James never said anything to me about that."

"He didn't need to but I am sure it manifested in other ways. You were never supposed to make it without him yet you did."

"I only did it because of God. I didn't do it on my own."

"I know that."

"He kept saying that I thought that I was better than him. I never wanted to be better than him. I love him."

"I know you love him but unfortunately James hasn't reached the level that you are at in your relationship with the Lord. When you told him that you were leaving this time, he knew that you would never come back to him again. The fear that you used to have was gone for good."

"You're right. I mean when he started calling me those names, I became really angry. I was pissed off because I know that is not who I am. I am not a bitch and a whore and I would be damned if I allow anyone to call me that. Excuse my French. I am fearfully and wonderfully made and will not accept anything less than that."

"That's right."

"He had the nerve to tell me that I wasn't a prize. How could he say that?"

"He said it because he had to see your reaction. In the past, you wouldn't have stood up to him like that."

"You're right. I know in my heart that if I would have flinched or cowered just a little bit, things would have been very bad. I felt the fear, I smelled it. Do you know what fear smells like? What am I saying. Of course you do."

"Yes, I know what it feels like. I also know what the joy of the Lord feels like too, and so do you. That's why I know that you will be just fine."

"I thank God." Jaynie's expression took on a somber look. "But what about Lance? He was so angry. In that instance, my baby grew up into a man. "

"Yes, he did and I am sure that he will be fine. That was a defining moment for him but God has had his hand on Lance's life for a long time. He will be fine."

"But I wanted him to know his father. I wanted him to grow up with James in his life."

"In time, James can be in his life but it is best that it is not now."

"I know. So what do I do? I told my sister that I will stay with her but right now I need some quiet time. You know, just to get my thoughts together."

"I know. I know a place that will be perfect for you."

"Is it a shelter because I really don't want to go to a shelter?"

"It's not a shelter. It's better than that. It's a safe haven for women. In fact, the owner, Kayla, came through our counseling program at the church around the same time that I did. It's funny but we each had to make up a plan for our lifetime. Kayla dreamed of her safe haven for women and I dreamed of Women of Destiny."

"So what's so special about her place?"

"Jaynie, I cannot even explain it to you. You have to experience it for yourself. Just know that God is truly awesome."

"I do."

"So this is what we will do. I will speak to Benjamin and let him know that we are going to have a ladies' weekend. I'll give Kayla a call and tell her that we are coming."

"Will Benjamin mind that you will be gone this weekend?"

"No, baby. He will be fine. He knows Kayla and loves her like a sister. He also knows me and is secure enough in our relationship to know that I am coming home. This will give him time with the children and with his friends. There was a time when he needed to know my every move but not now. I promise you that the Holy Spirit is all up in our marriage and will convict either of us if we did wrong."

"That's' good. James would never let that happen."

"James's trust in you is low because he doesn't have a relationship with God. But let's not think about that right now. Let's just concentrate on having a good time."

"That's fine."

"Besides Benjamin knows that I won't turn down the opportunity to visit the Soul."

"The Soul?"

"That's right. When Kayla first dreamed of this place, it was called Soul's Simplicities. She wanted to include all the simplicities of life that made life worth living. It needed to be filled with love, peace, and joy. But of course, we shortened the name to the Soul."

"Wow."

"That's not it. I don't want to give it away because you will have to see it to believe it. But Kayla thought of every detail to give women hope. You know, like I know, that it can be very hard to leave an abusive relationship. A woman's self esteem is damaged. In times, many women return to their abusive situations because, let's be real, it is very difficult to make it on your own. The husband has been the bread winner or provided the medical care. Even if the woman has a job, it is usually not one that can evoke independence. Therefore, it is easy to return back or better yet, to never leave."

"I know. I was so afraid to make it on my own. I never knew how dependent I was on James."

"And you have a good job. But it's not just about money. It boils down to how we feel about ourselves."

"When we know who we are and we know whose we are, we are less apt to settle for less." Kayla and Minister Alexander chimed in together to recite the anthem of Women of Destiny.

"When I think about God and the plan that he had for my life, before I was even born, I can't help but to get excited." Minister Alexander continued. "Who would have thought that my life with Benjamin would have developed into something like this. I wanted to leave but God would not help me. How was I able to sleep at night in that house of hell? God's angels were all encamped around me. Now, I am leading other women into their destiny and Benjamin is leading other men into their rightful place. Only God can do this."

"Praise the lord."

"That's what I am saying. But you also know what, Jaynie. We each have our cross to bear. My life turned out this way because God needed for me to use my testimony to help others. It took me a long time to become transparent. I still get nervous when I tell my story."

"Oh, I think about the day when I sat in the auditorium and listened to you. I could not believe you were putting it out like that."

"I had to. Domestic violence has to stop. The only way this is going to be possible is if men and women step up and call it for what it is. A trap of the devil."

"When you tell your story, it still gives me chills." Jaynie admitted.

"It gives me chills to because I have to relive it each time. The memories are there but the pain is gone." Minister Alexander continues. "God never asks us to forget. He asks us to trust him enough to bring us through. I believe that we should never forget where we came from. Unfortunately, there are too many people who choose to live in the sea of forgetfulness. But in order to confront the issue, we need to face it and peel back all the layers."

"I understand."

"Abuse is the after fact. There are underlying issues in both the abuser and the abused that keep them in this cycle of violence. Once you peel back all the layers, you will find that underneath the anger is fear, insecurity, and low self-esteem. The same is true for those who are addicted to alcohol, drugs, sex, and shopping."

"Shopping?"

"That's right. Simple things such as shopping, gambling, and lying are products of insecurity and fear. Think about it this way. There is no way that someone would put themselves in financial debt just for a pair of Jimmy Choos. It happens all the time though. It's a sickness and it's a trap."

"I see."

"This is what we are going to do. You are going to follow me to my house so that I can pack. We'll check up on Lance to see how he is doing. Then we are on our way to the Soul for some relaxation, peace, and sister love."

"Hey, Benjamin. How are you doing?"

"I'm blessed, Jaynie. What about you?"

"I'm here."

Benjamin and Jaynie were making small talk while Kim was packing.

"Jaynie, I'm sorry about everything. Is there anything that I can do?"

"No, there isn't, but thanks for offering." Jaynie thought about it. "If you could possibly talk to Lance, I would appreciate it very much. Right now, he is going to need positive male role models."

"Consider it done. Where is he at now?" Benjamin asked.

"He's with his best friend Tony. He'll be there while we are gone."

"I'll check on him when you come back."

"Thanks. I will appreciate that a lot. You and Kim have been a great support."

"Why, thanks. We only do what we can."

"Well, in case I haven't told you this before, you have been a blessing to me."

"Thanks. Anytime you need to talk, then give me a call."

Jaynie pondered her next question.

"Benjamin, can I ask you a question?"

"Yes, shoot."

"Why did you do all the things that you did? Minister Alexander is a wonderful woman. How could you hurt her in such a way?"

"To be honest, at that time, I just didn't care. I was hurting and unfortunately I was only thinking about me."

"But you didn't just hit her once; you did it for over twenty years. What made you stop?"

"Kim made me look at myself. That day when she stood outside of our house for all of our neighbors to see, she brought all of our darkness to light. Up until that day, I could always pretend that everything was a figment of her imagination. Yeah, I admitted to hitting her but it was never in a spot that was so visible. I could always say that she made me do it. You know, make her feel crazy."

"But when she stood out on the street and then went to work, there was no way that I could explain myself out of it. Her family and friends knew. Her boss and my boss. People were talking."

"So you mean to tell me that you were embarrassed only when she shared your life with the world. Why weren't you embarrassed and shameful from the beginning? Why did things have to get so bad?"

"Bad. That wasn't even the half of it. Kim had the audacity to stay in the house. I wanted her to leave. At least then, I could still talk myself out of the fact that I was an abuser. I used Kim in every possible way. I took advantage of her in ways that she may never share. And through it all, she still continued to care for me. She still continued to love me when I didn't even love myself. It is so easy to hurt others when you are hurting yourself."

"So what changed? When did you finally wake up?"

"Let me see. It was as clear as day. Kim came in one day from work and I swear there was a glow surrounding her. I had never seen it before. She was laughing and smiling. Her eyes were on fire."

"I kept asking her what was up. What was she so happy about? In the back of my mind, I kept thinking that she had finally met another man, one who was worthy of her love. I still didn't think that I deserved her. I started accusing her of cheating. And you know what she did. She laughed in my face. Then she went to bed. I mean here I was yelling and screaming and she had the nerve to go to sleep. Just like that."

"So what did you do?"

"I ranted and raved. I drank all the liquor in the house. I cursed and screamed. Each time I went into the bedroom, I would check, and sure enough she was sleep. How she was able to sleep in such chaos amazed me. It also angered me."

"So what happened?"

"The next morning Kim woke up as early as ever and fixed me breakfast. I tried to ask her about the night before but she only silenced me by placing her finger to my lips. Every time I tried to speak, she would silence me. Never yelling or being confrontational. Just full of peace. Then she said out loud, to no one in particular, "It is finished. Thank you Lord.""

"So what did it all mean?"

"At the time, I could not figure it out but now that I am a bit wiser. I realized that at that moment my wife had turned my life back over to God. You see, she let me go. I know you have heard the saying, 'Let go and let God.' Well, when Kim turned me back over to the Lord, I was scared. I mean up until that moment, her prayers protected me from the wrath of god. I know this now. He gave me mercy because of her. She was supposed to sit under my covering but I let her down. I failed as her husband. Yet, through it all, he spared me. However, that day she put her hands up and gave up the fight. I was left to fight with my own self and my own demons."

"Wow, I have never heard of this."

"Exactly. A husband's role is to cover his wife just as God covers us. I failed in my role. I didn't cover my wife. Instead, I hurt her in every way imaginable. I did not value her as the child of God that she is. Not only is she my wife but she is also my sister in Christ. Yes, I knew it was wrong. All the times that I called her out of her name left me in shame. All the times that I hit, punched, or slapped her made me sick with guilt. I can never take back those memories but I can do my best to erase them. Each day I thank God for her that she was able to love me still. She loved me with the same love that

Christ had. I realize that the glow that encompassed her was God's glory itself. She was able to sleep in peace because she was resting in the Lord to take over and reign. She gave it all up to him and he has blessed us both."

Jaynie sat still and began to reflect on her life. She realized that at that moment, she was nowhere near the place that Minister Alexander had come to. Yes, she loved James but she had not relinquished her control over the situation. She wanted James to change but realized that she herself needed to change. She needed a renewed mind.

"Jaynie, please don't think that our situation is perfect. Each day is still a struggle because we are mere humans. God's plan for our lives may be very different than God's plan for your life, with or without James."

"I understand."

"There isn't a day that goes by when Kim doesn't talk about you and the accomplishments that you have made. Please don't ever forget who you are and where you are. God's plan for our lives is so much greater than the plan that we have for ourselves."

"I know what you mean but can you please tell me the plan that he has for me. I know he told me to go back home yet I sit in your living room without a place to go."

"Do you ever think that he told you to go home so that you can he can prove to you that he is still God?"

"I don't get it."

"You see, God has an awesome plan for your life. Of all the women who have passed through Women of Destiny, you are the only one who has remained faithful. You and my wife. You have not only understood the process of forgiveness but you are a living example of it. You chose to go home and love James in spite of himself. I'm sorry that he could not see that because you are an amazing woman."

"Although you made tremendous progress in the group, you still held on to regret that you took Lance and left James the first time.

You cannot fully serve the Lord if there is any type of resentment in your heart. So God needed to send you back so that you could make a choice."

"Keep going, please."

"He had given you a taste of His glory before you went back to James yet you still wondered if it was worth it. He allowed you to return to show you that there is no substitute to the love that he has for his sons and daughters. You already knew who you were and whose you were. That is why you refused to let James address you in any manner unworthy of your name."

"I know what you mean. I was so angry when he said that I wasn't a prize. I mean how could he say such a thing?"

"It was easy for him because this is all be knows. He doesn't know any better. Only a man of God would recognize your spirit because he would be operating through his spirit. Unfortunately, James isn't operating that way. He only knows you based on your past."

"But it wasn't like I was trifling in my past."

"I am not saying that you were. What I meant to say is that in the past you operated a different way. When James would talk down to you, you usually allowed him to. Even if you chose to argue with him, he could always remind you of your past. Your argument would lose its validity. But now, praise God, you know who you are and will not let anyone degrade you ever again. You actually took a stand and fought for yours."

"I don't know. When I moved back home, things started out wonderfully. James and I came to church on a consistent basis but then things started to change. The closer I got into the word, the more angrier he became."

"That was because you were relying on something that you could not see versus relying on him. Just know that it could have been anything that would have made him angry and jealous. A friend, your job, the Lord. James realized that your relationship with God was more important than your relationship with him."

"But I never intended it to be. I love James so much. I wanted us to both grow in the Lord."

"I understand that. But what you fail to realize is that each person must come to the Lord on their own. When Kim threw her hands up on that day, it was as if she was saying, "Lord, I'll go if I have to go, by myself." She made the choice between life and death and I have mad respect for her now. At that time, I couldn't see it."

"So what made you change your mind? Did you change for Kim?"

"No. The last thing I was going to do was change for her. To me that would have meant giving up my power and control. No, God had to work on me his own way."

"So what did he do?"

"Everything and everyone around me seemed to have this flow going on while I was falling apart. Aside from the drinking, I had given up in other ways. In case you didn't know it, many men carry the guilt and shame of being abusers. When people know, they will judge; even if they feign impartiality. It was hard having to explain myself. Kim was a good woman and everyone around us knew that so it was very difficult for me to place blame."

"How could you blame her in the first place? She didn't hit you. You hit her."

"Yes, I did hit her. But you have to understand that I made excuses for myself and I blamed her. Why didn't she just do right? Why didn't she just listen to me in the first place? It didn't help with the fact that Kim never challenged me; instead she worked harder to please me. It's a sick cycle."

"Yes, it is and I cannot believe that I left it once and still came back to it again."

"You can't keep blaming yourself. A dog will keep going back to its own vomit. You didn't know any better. You didn't have a choice."

"Yes, I did. I could have stayed away."

"If only. The reason I say that you did not have a choice is because you hadn't known of anything to make you think differently. That's why I love my men's group. I wasn't sure of the response that we would have considering our choice of topic. Not too many men want to admit that they lose control. Yes, domestic abuse is about losing control."

"I'm not getting that. I mean the man is controlling the women by abusing her."

"Yes, that's true but the underlying reason for his abuse has to deal with him losing control through his fear, insecurity, loneliness, and frustration. He's afraid because he realizes that one day his woman is going to wake up and leave. It's inevitable. He's insecure because he realizes that the only way that he can keep his woman there is to dominate her. He doesn't know how to keep her satisfied with kind words, devotion, and more than likely, good loving. Let's be real. If a woman is satisfied, then she will take care of her home and her man and combat any issues. He's lonely because nine times out of ten, he does not have a close group of friends that he can seek counsel with. He is too afraid to let anyone in because then they will then be privy to his shortcomings. He is frustrated because he realizes that nothing, absolutely nothing, is working."

"Wow, you have given me a lot to think about. I thank you for sharing this with me."

"It's no problem. God is good. One day Kim came home from church with an ultimatum. I either attend the Brothers Helping Brothers support group or leave the house. She said that I was stealing her joy. I tried protesting but it didn't work. I knew she was right. So I started attending group at the church. It was hard at first because the men wouldn't cut me any slack. However, once I started being honest with myself and became accountable to my brothers in the group, my life changed. Hallelujah."

"You know something Benjamin. I never shared this with anyone other than your wife. You two were my inspiration and one of the reasons that I chose to go home. Your passion for the Lord is incredible. However, I realize that your life together and purpose had been orchestrated for you two alone. My life with James is of no comparison because our passions are not tied up into the Lord. Therefore, let two who are unequally yoked…

"That's right."

"And the bottom line of this all is that James and I were not even married. We were living together which is sin altogether. We were playing house on a foundation that was not rooted in the Lord and his commandments. God is not going to honor that, let's be real."

"Exactly."

"That's why we had to separate. Yet, James did not understand. My hope was that we would part and then come back together the right way. But now that is not going to happen. A part of me is sad, don't get me wrong, yet another part of me is thankful that God's plans for me as so much better than the plans that I have for myself."

"Praise God."

"Hallelujah."

Jaynie was finally coming into revelation knowledge. A threefold cord cannot be easily broken. If God is in the midst, then you can do the impossible. If God is no where around, it is impossible.

"What is going on in here? Are you two having church without me?" Minister Alexander entered the living room.

"Hey baby. Jaynie and I were just talking. Do you have everything packed for your weekend in paradise?"

"Yes, sir. I do. Everything except you."

"See, you just had to go there. Getting me all worked up so that you can leave me."

"I know. That's my plan. You need not forget who I am."

"I never can. I never will." Benjamin held out his arms for Kim. "Come here, sweetie and give me a hug."

"Jaynie, will you excuse us please. I need to make some memories with my husband."

Blushing, Jaynie responded quickly, "Not a problem at all. I'll wait for you in the car. Let me get your bag." Jaynie reached for the duffel bag.

"Sweetie, don't worry about that. I'll bring it." Benjamin interjected. "You go ahead to the car."

"That's right Jaynie. He's the man. Let him do it. That's his purpose. To take care of the women in his life."

Jaynie walked out with a smile on her face.

"That sounded kind of chauvinistic, my dear."

"It wasn't chauvinistic. It was the truth. Don't let me go show you the scripture." Kim began to walk away from Benjamin.

"Where do you think you're going? I know you are not walking away from me now. We're supposed to be making memories, did you forget."

"You're right, baby. I'm sorry." Kim kissed her husband on the forehead. "So tell me, are you going to miss me as much as I am going to miss you."

"Of course I am. We haven't been apart in a long time. But it's cool because I understand why you are leaving."

"I know. I just wanted to help Jaynie out. This is going to be a tough journey for her and the Soul is the best place for her to be."

"I know it is. I also know that you need this as much as she does."

"What do you mean?"

"You don't remember, do you?"

"No."

"When we were together before I was saved, I never wanted you to leave my side. One reason was because I thought you would never come back. Let's be real, I wasn't the best person to be around. I hurt you really bad."

"Yes, that's true. But things are so much better between us."

"That's because God is in our lives. We have submitted ourselves to serving him first, which is why we can serve one another."

"Keep preaching, baby."

"When you walked into the house on that day when I was given another chance to live, I asked you if you had found another man. Don't' you remember? You just smiled at me without answering."

"I couldn't answer you. There was no way that you would have understood where I was at in that moment. I had an encounter with God when I finally let you go. Up until then, I worshipped you and lived my life according to your will. Not His. That was so wrong. Yet, God revealed himself to me and I came out from under you and found peace in Him."

"Your soul was at peace."

"Yes, it was. All the abuse and pain went away. All the hurt and fear vanished. My past was erased. Guilt and shame had to flee. You see, even though I stayed in the house with you, I still misunderstood the purpose of it all. Yet God made it so clear to me that day. Once I gave him total praise for all the crap that I had been through, he was able to release my soul and set me free."

"The Soul is about release and total surrender to the will of God," Benjamin spoke. "That's why you need to go just as much as Jaynie. We all need to get to that place in our lives where we can give it all to the Lord and totally surrender to his will. Not just once but forever more."

"Amen, baby, amen. I love it when you preach. Come here and give me my kiss. I love you so much."

"I love you too."

Benjamin kissed his wife with as much passion as he could muster. Who would have thought that twenty two years of hell could be replaced by five years of heaven? Holding his wife in his arms never felt better.

"Thank you God", he silently whispered.

Kim rested in the peace of her joy. Who would have thought that the one man that she feared for twenty years, would grow into such a faithful man of God.

"Thank you God," she silently whispered.

"Girl, get over here and give me a hug" Kayla heartily greeted Celeste. "Look at you, all dressed up in your uniform serving the community."

"Look at the pot calling the kettle black." Celeste countered. "Talk about serving the community. You are definitely doing it up. This place is truly awesome."

"Yes it is. Yes it is." Kayla agreed. "I thank God every day for allowing this to all happen."

"I know. This house is definitely going to save a lot of souls."

"I know but it's more than the house. How beautiful it is no comparison to how good God is. When I say that I thank God for allowing it to happen, I mean the abuse and everything. It made me who I am today."

"That's right. A strong, beautiful, awesome women of God."

"Why thank you, my dear." Kayla graciously accepted the praise from her dear friend.

"It's my pleasure. I knew you were special when I first met you. I know that it wasn't under the best circumstances but something in my spirit told me that you were going to be just fine."

"It was a long way to travel but I am finally home." Kayla sat in reflection. "Hey, Celeste, I never had the opportunity to tell you thank you for bringing Jennifer to my home. She is my very first guest."

"Yes she is. I just love how you say that she is your guest. It will make her feel welcomed."

"I know. It can be a very scary to walk away from abuser."

"How come? I mean how difficult can it be to walk away from someone who is bashing your head in. Why would a person choose to stay?"

Although Celeste was being harsh, Kayla couldn't get angry. There are so many people who feel just as she does.

"Celeste, what you fail to realize is that choice is something that victims feel that they don't have. When a woman is being abused, whether it is mentally, physically, or emotionally, she feels as if she has no control over the situation. She is powerless to make it stop. Why do I say that? I say that because there are too many cases where women choose to stay in a bad situation, even when they are offered a way out."

"I know. There have been times when I have been called to a house for a domestic violence situation and the woman is as bloody as ever. Yet, when I offer to take her to a shelter, she refuses. It makes me so mad."

"She refuses because she has come to believe that her sole purpose in life is to take care of her abuser, whether it is her husband or boyfriend. Therefore, choosing differently is not an option." Kayla answered.

"Abuse is subtle," Kayla continued. "Nine times out of ten, her significant other did not meet her, say "I love you", and then bash her head in. No, it is a gradual process that first starts with destroying her sense of rationality. A woman begins to second guess herself more often than not. Did he really say that? Is my mind playing tricks on me? I know he yelled but was it directed to me or is this a result of the situation that he is in. His job. His finances. Her man could have called her stupid or maybe even grabbed her arm. If she questions his actions yet doesn't react, then he realizes that even though he has crossed the line, her boundaries aren't too difficult to penetrate. Think about it this way. If a person walked up to you and snatched your purse, I promise you that won't second guess the situation. If a total stranger walked up to you and called you a bitch, nine times out of ten, you would be ready to whup his tail. You will not be disrespected like that by anybody."

"You are absolutely right."

"However, things are different when two people enter into a relationship. Some women may allow one, maybe two times for a brother to have a lapse of reality and then it's on. Still there are others that won't take such a strong stand. They will overlook the issue and pretend that it didn't happen. Unfortunately for them, this gives the abuser another time to cross the boundary. The next time is worse than the last but it is not as worse as it could be."

"So why doesn't she leave?"

"In my opinion, a woman doesn't leave because she comes to a crossroad, yet, remains still. She doesn't make a decision because each option poses risks. If she leaves him, then she may have to endure real life issues such as financial difficulties, finding a place to live, or living in constant fear of retaliation. Then, there are other underlying issues that she may face such as low self-esteem, feeling inadequate or as a failure, and unworthiness. Of course, if she stays, she will still have to endure the physical abuse, along with, feeling as if she deserved it in some way. Making the decision to leave is very difficult. As bad as a situation can be, there is a sense of familiarity. She knows her mate. I know that I shouldn't simplify it but it boils down to this. Does she have enough faith to realize that God does not what her to live in a hell where she is degraded and dead but instead wants her to trust him enough to come out and choose life?"

"So what you are trying to say is that some women feel that living in their present situation is better than stepping out on faith and living in the unknown."

"Yes, that is what I am saying. I know for me that I was very afraid of living alone and starting all over again. No matter how bad things got between Tyson and me, it was still my world and I had some control over it. Yes, I jumped through hoops to please him but some days I was able to get it right. To me, as long as we weren't fighting, then things were all good. I hadn't realized that there were other ways that I was dying a slow death. The scripture says "He whom the son sets free, shall be free indeed."

"That's right."

"But during that time, I wasn't in the word. I was hiding from the world and hiding from the Lord. I wasn't free to be myself in the relationship because I couldn't freely voice my opinion when something was wrong for fear that we would argue. I couldn't freely go and do things that were of interest to me. I couldn't express my emotions, whether it was to be happy, sad, or silly. I wasn't free to be who God intended for me to be."

"I look at you now and I cannot imagine why someone would hurt you in such a way." Celeste revealed. "But not just you. There are many women who I have met that have the sweetest souls. I just don't get it."

"There was a time when I didn't get it either. Each time we argued or fought, I felt drained in every way. I think that mentally, I was gone. I was constantly thinking for so many years that getting eight hours of sleep was a joke. I functioned on four. I don't think anyone understands how exhausting it is to overthink a situation, especially when your life depended on it. You find yourself constantly asking, Is this going to be the day when he kills me? Should I fight him to my death or thank God for it?"

"Wow, I can't say that I know what it feels like."

"I just thank God that I didn't have any kids," Kayla shamelessly admitted. "I would never want them to go through this. But then on the other hand, I found myself asking why I couldn't stop my own self from going through it. What was wrong with me?"

"Ooh, Kayla. You are really getting to me."

"I know I am. I would apologize but I can't. I thank God that I can talk about my situation. I should have been dead a long time ago but he chose to keep me here. At first, I asked God to just take me and let me die. Since he wasn't going to take me out of the situation, then he could at least grant me my last request. I even asked God to take Tyson out. I know its bad to wish death on someone, but as much as I loved him, I also hated him. I trusted him with all that I had and he still didn't want me. All he had to do was love me or at least pretend that he did. Now if that ain't a shameful thing to say then I don't know what is."

"So what made you come out of this?"

"I had to get real. When I first left Tyson, I went to meetings through the Domestic Violence Hotline. There I met so many women who were in my same situation. It was a wake up call for me because we each told the same story although we were all different. The sad thing about it is for that one hour when we met, we were able to open up and share our situations with one another without any shame or guilt. We offered our opinions and said, "Girl, you should have left him a long time ago", while in the back of our minds, we asked, "Why didn't I leave him a long time ago." We laughed and shared stories of times long ago when we were happy and running carefree. Then we cried for the realities of our situations and prayed that we would be able to meet once again. We never knew who would come back the following week or go into hiding."

"Do you still hear from any of the women in your group?"

"Yes, I have seen some. Depending on the situation, we will offer eye contact if their abuser is still around or we will embrace one another knowing that no matter how close we are for that one hour, there are still 23 more hours to go."

"I have a few close friends and I cannot imagine letting a week go by without speaking to them."

"That's all good. You see, those counseling services were very helpful to many women. I thank God for being able to attend them. However, there came a time when we each needed to move on. I think I hung around there for two years because it was such a comfort. But eventually, I had to move on." Kayla took a deep sigh as she reflection on that time in her life. "That is the scariest part of it all because no matter how many tools and resources they had tried to supply, having to come back into society was totally different. There were so many unanswered questions, such as, *Can I or should I ever trust again? I have been used and abused, who will ever want me? Why me?* and *Where do I go from here?* Again, you are overthinking your situation and can sometimes freeze up to the idea of new relationships. I know I sound like a broken record, but the Lord is so good. When you learn to trust in him, all fear has to leave. When you realize that you can come to him, used and abused, and he will still wants you, low self-esteem has to flee. When you find out that he can take your bad situation and use it for good, it opens you up to new possibilities. Hmmph, now you got me preaching all up in here." Kayla felt a chill rum up her spine.

"It's all good because you are enlightening me."

"So once I started leaning on the Lord and resting in him, my life began to turn around. I began to take an inventory of myself and I found out that I am not that bad. For a long time, I felt that there was something wrong with me. But, thank goodness, I am not there anymore. It's been a long road well traveled but I believe that I am now living in my destiny."

"Your destiny?"

"Yes. Before I was born, God knew all about me. He knew all that I would endure, the good, the bad, and the ugly. I have made peace with the knowledge that I was able to endure all that I have, without long lasting scars, for this purpose right here. To take care of those who need me. For a long time, I hated who I was. It seemed as if I was always giving while someone was always taking."

"Do you think that this has affected you?"

"Of course it has. For a long time, I felt that I always got the short end of the stick. I felt responsible to those around me and always placed them before myself. No matter how hard I tried to say no, it was as if no one heard me. But you know what I have learned is that being a giver is not as bad as it can be. God lets us know that it is better to give than to receive."

"Yeah, I know that. But there has to be a time when you have to put your foot down. To keep giving to someone that is unappreciative is just plain wrong. Enough is enough."

"Exactly. That is why I learned to accept who I am. I am a giver and would not want it any other way. Therefore, if I have my last and you need it, then so be it. It's yours. I finally let go of the resentment that I had toward those who were taking from me and began examining my heart. I needed to question my intentions and search my heart. I realized that my intentions weren't always pure. I say this because my actions were dependent on a person's reaction. If they did not acknowledge my efforts, then I was hurt. If they did acknowledge my efforts, then my day went well. Their response to me dictated my whole day. If my actions were pure from the beginning, then it would not have bothered me so much if I did not receive an adequate response. I would have been able to move on without any regrets."

Kayla continued, "I had to ask God to show me my heart and he did. Once I came to him and put it on the line, my pride, my intentions, he allowed me to see that I needed to accept the fact that I am indeed a giver. Unfortunately, I had not used discretion in my decision makings. I began to pray to God to teach me discernment so that I could give to those who truly needed help and could walk away from those who did not have a pure heart. And you know what?"

"No, what?"

"It came to me in a flash. This idea of setting up a shelter in my home where I can offer support to women who need it. It is working out perfectly because I can still give to others in such a way that my intentions can only be pure. This is very risky because I am dealing with complete strangers who are going through a whirlwind of events. However, I have enough faith in my God to know that everything will fall into place because my intentions are to help these women grow into the women that they are called to be. By taking me and my feelings out of the equation, God can do all his wonderful things."

"You have definitely given me something to think about. Because I have never been in your shoes, I came in with a "If that was me…" kind of attitude. That was totally wrong of me and I apologize. I cannot begin to understand the psychological effects that domestic violence can have on a person."

"Yes, it can be devastating, however, what I want others to learn is that nothing is impossible when you have the Lord in your life. He can turn those dark situations around in an instant, especially when you come to him with a pure heart. This goes for the women who are abused and their abusers."

Celeste looked at Kayla quizzically, "What I am still trying to understand is why you would even care about the men who have done these bad things. The way I see it is that it's their fault anyway."

"I hear what you are saying. In my situation, Tyson was the one who came after me. There are things that went on between us that only God knows. However, I have to be honest. There were also times between us that were very good. Nevertheless, abuse is a cycle that has been repeated for many generations. I refuse to believe that I was the lucky one, the one who caused him to lose control and hit me. Oh no. there is history of it."

"Why are you so sure?"

"I am sure because I have learned some things over the years. Abuse is abuse yet it comes in many different forms. Physical seems to be the most horrific because we can actually see the bruises and scars. However, we cannot forget emotional abuse, financial control, mental cruelty, neglect, silent treatment, abandonment and control through guilt. These manifestations are just as bad. However, their root comes from feeling inadequate, being hurt and afraid, feeling unloved, and insecurity. If we dig back the layers of our lives, we will find that these feelings were rooted into our childhood. Unfortunately, we may not have been taught how to address them in healthy ways. Therefore, hurt people hurt other people." Kayla looked at Celeste for her reaction. "Maybe I should not simplify it in such a manner."

"Keep going. I am learning."

"However, the only way that a person can heal from the inside out is if they can peel back these layers and expose themselves. There aren't too many people who are willing to do that. It hurts too much. For this reason, I have had to put my bitterness in check and not place blame. I have come close to death on many occasions but God spared my life. I had to become transparent. It's the only way that I can help others."

"So how can you possibly help the men? They cannot very well come here."

"No they cannot. However, there are many organization out there where there are brothers who have been in the same situation and came out of it. They have become transparent and will share their testimony with anyone. My concern is with the women. Of course, I can only deal with a few women at a time. But that's OK. If I can be an example to them and help them heal, I am sure that they can do the same for others. Sort of like the domino effect. Eventually it can grow in to something bigger than you or me. Generational curses can be broken. Children's' lives can be changed."

Celeste held out her hand. "Kayla, please stop. You're getting me all pumped up."

"Girl, I can't help it. God has been moving in my life in such a way that I find myself pinching myself at night. Look at this." Kayla spread her arms out throughout the house. "Look at me. Celeste, you know the deal."

"Of course I do. I still cannot believe what Tyson did."

"Why can't you. There were many things that went on between us."

"I know. But Kayla, let's be real. He hit you with his car."

"Yes he did."

"And on top of that, he didn't just do it one time. He did it twice."

"Yes he did."

"What I still can't understand is that you never even tried to prosecute him. All you needed to do was to press charges and we could have been all over him. We still can, you know."

"I know that. But I couldn't press charges. What happened between Tyson and me spanned over twelve years. Hitting me with the car was the least of it. I can say that because at that time in my life, I was resting in the arms of the Lord."

"What do you mean?"

"You see, for several months before that incident, I had actually began planning my escape. In fact, I can tell you the exact day that I began to do so. It was November 17, 2001. Tyson and I had just had a major blowout, over God knows what. He was tripping as usual." Kayla stared off reflectively. "Anyway," she continued, "on that particular day, I had been feeling out of sorts. I was very anxious, more than usual. I made sure that the house was spotless, dinner was on the stove. I had gotten dressed and made sure that all the bases were covered. But Tyson never came home."

"Why not?"

"To this day, I don't know why. I remember waiting for several hours, wondering if he would walk through the door. A part of me was scared that he would never return and I would be alone. Another part of me was glad that he might not come home and I would be alone. Nevertheless, I struggled with my emotions. Ain't that crazy. I was actually having mixed feelings about the situation."

"For hours, I laughed and I cried." Kayla continued. "I laid in bed balled up in the fetal position and that's when I saw it."

"What did you see?"

"I saw my bible. It was tattered and torn, but not from my reading it. My grandma gave me that bible several years ago. I remember spending my days with her as a young girl. Ma Dear would sit outside on her front porch with her bible laid across her lap. She would fan the flies away and gaze off down the block, rocking ever so gently on the porch swing. She would always recite her favorite bible verses. Psalm 27 was her favorite. *The lord is my light and my salvation.*"

"God is so good, isn't He," Celeste chimed in.

"Yes, He is and let me tell you how", Kayla continued. "Sure enough I picked up her bible that night and I opened it directly to Psalm 27. "It was as if my grandma was speaking straight to my soul. I read that passage and knew that I had forgotten all that she had taught me. My grandma was God fearing only. No man, woman or thing on earth could frighten her because she knew that she had the Lord on her side. That very moment, I prayed and asked God for forgiveness. Forgiveness for leaving Him. Forgiveness for wishing that Tyson would never return. Forgiveness for not trusting in the Lord to help me make a way. I prayed all through the house that night and curled up in bed and rested in my Daddy's arms. My life was a mess, I knew it. I made some bad decisions in my life and chose the wrong people to surround me."

"So what happened? Did Tyson come back?"

"Of course he did. No sooner had I fallen off to sleep, Tyson came in in rarer form than when he left. He came into the bedroom and began calling my name. "Kayla, Kayla, are you asleep. Wake up." Now I was asleep, finally I was asleep, but you know what he did, he kept calling me." Lord, make him stop." I begged. But nothing happened. "Kayla, wake up." All of saddened, whoosh, the covers came off of me. I lay uncovered in the bed just as I was uncovered in our relationship. "Kayla, I know you hear me."

"I remember asking him if he could let me sleep," Kayla continued to recall.

"What did he say?"

"He said, "No". He wanted to talk. Mind you it had to be 4 o'clock in the morning."

"I tried to lay still but Tyson was on a roll. He grabbed my feet and pulled me directly out of the bed. I landed straight on my back."

"You know you hear me, Kayla. Stop playing," he said.

"At that very moment, I saw it so clearly. Tyson could care less about how I felt or what I needed. Back then, I was getting by with only four or five hours of sleep, never restful. Yet on that very day, I was resting like a baby in God's arms and he ripped me from them."

"Why didn't you just tell him No" Celeste asked.

"You know, when I think about it, I could have said something. But you have to remember that I was afraid to ever go against him. I always hoped that one day he would actually see his actions and apologize, but it never happened. I continued to pray to God but it was always in silence, in my mind. I know that we should boldly proclaim His name but I was just happy enough to whisper it in my heart."

"But how did you plan your escape?"

"Girl, each day, I would set aside a few more clothes, a few more dollars. Yeah, I was working and all of that, but Tyson knew how much I got paid and when I got paid. He needed to make sure that I was able to contribute my part to all of the finances. Up until that point, I never questioned that what was mine, was ours. In my eyes, I felt that we were family. Tyson also believed that what was mine was ours, but not vice versa. He worked but it wasn't nearly enough to pay all of the bills. Therefore, I paid the bulk of the bills. That is until I left." Kayla continued to explain her situation.

Curiosity was getting to Celeste, "I hear you but I am waiting to hear how you planned your escape."

"Let's see, I had visited several apartments and filled out applications. Each time I went, I was sure to explain my situation. I knew that it could be risky because many apartments would not want such a drama on their property. Anything could happen. Nevertheless, I explained my plight to the agents. "Look, I'm going to be real with you. I need to leave my ex and I need a place to stay." For a long time, no one bit. Until one day, thank you God, this woman named Patti decided to take me up on my offer. Before I could even give my practiced speech, Patti interrupted me."

"Baby, you don't have to explain anything to me. Believe me when I tell you that I understand what you are going through. I've been there."

Chills ran through Kayla and Celeste's bodies. "Let me tell you, I was shocked. I couldn't even speak," Kayla admitted.

"Don't worry sweetie," Patti continued. "I have been waking up every morning at about 3:14. Each time I found myself praying for peace for someone, yet I could never put a face to him or her. But when you walked into the door, I knew that it must have been you. Are you ready to move today?"

"Well, uh."

"You didn't expect to hear yes, did you?" Patti asked knowingly.

"No," Kayla shyly admitted.

"Why not, baby? Don't you know that with God, it is only Yes and Amen. I may have a few years over you but just know that I have been there. This is what I want you to do. I want you to go home and think about all of this. Are you ready to be free? If so, here is my card." Patti passed her card to Kayla. "Call me anytime and I will have you an apartment, either here or somewhere else."

"Are you serious?"

"Yes ma'am, I am."

"So did you leave at that moment?" Celeste eagerly asked.

"No, girl, I was scared. I knew that I asked God to help me, but I never knew it was going to be that quick. Anyway, I went home that night feeling quite shaken but with a different attitude. I knew that I needed to think fast and move fast. I walked into our house hoping that Tyson wasn't there. But he was."

"So what happened?"

"He had a rough day at work, at least that's what he said. Anyway, he started up as soon as I came in." Kayla recounted that fateful day.

"Oh, I see you finally made it in. Where were you?"

"I went out for a little while. It was nothing."

"It must have been something since you weren't here when I came home. Where were you, Kayla."

"I was out. It wasn't important." I walked to the sink and began washing my hands. Tyson was quiet for a long but I knew that he was thinking. You see, any other time, I would give him a rundown of my day without hesitation. It was easier that way. If not, he would wake me up in the middle of the night to question me. He said that it would be hard for me to lie then, since I would be so sleepy."

"Shoot, girl. He was really playing mind tricks on you," Celeste added.

"That's right. I was mentally exhausted. Anyway, he was cool but I knew that things were far from over. I remember praying to God that He wouldn't let us fight. I was scared, too. The anticipation was the worse. We ate dinner in silence. I washed the dishes and put them away and then got ready for bed. That's when he started up. As I was in the shower, Tyson burst into the bathroom. I never expected him to do that since the bathroom seemed to be the only place where I could have peace."

"So what happened?"

"I was in the shower thanking God for letting me make it through another day. I was thinking about the offer that Patti had given me about the apartment. It was so tempting but I also realized that I was deathly afraid to make a move on my own. I just didn't think that I was capable."

"So…" Celeste waited with anticipation for Kayla to finish the story.

Kayla visibly began trembling as she recanted the story. "Tyson pulled back the curtains and just looked at me."

"Hey baby, what's the matter?' I cheerfully asked him.

"I'm waiting, Kayla."

"Waiting for what?"

"I'm waiting for you to tell me the truth. Something is up and I want to hear it now."

"Can you let me finish showering and then I will be out?"

"No."

"What do you mean, no. All I want to do is rinse off and then we can talk. I promise."

"No."

"Come on Tyson. I am serious. I am playing."

"I'm not playing either."

"I looked in his eyes and I knew that he was serious, dead serious. I tried to reach for the shower knob to cut off the water but Tyson grabbed my hand. You better start talking."

"Girl, I got to be real with you," Kayla continued. "I was scared. Here I was in the shower, completely naked, and Tyson was pissed off. I cannot even explain the fear. I thought about so many things. Was he going to hit me? I was soaking wet. Was he going to pinch me? Everything was exposed. Was he going to kill me? I was completely naked. I couldn't help praying. God, please get me out of here. Earlier that day I was hoping that he was dead but now I was unsure if I wanted to be dead myself."

"Kayla, you must think that I am stupid." Tyson continued.

"No, baby, I would never think that."

"Good because if you are trying to play me, you better remember that I can play harder and I play to win."

"I know."

Then he walked out of the bathroom.

Celeste interrupted. "I can only imagine what that was like. The intimidation and fear."

"True. When I walked out of the bathroom, I could not possibly rest. I kept waiting for him to snap. But he never did."

"No? Why not?"

"I don't know. It was at that moment that I knew that I couldn't test my fate anymore. I had to leave. I laid in bed that night being sure that I wouldn't move out of that one spot. I don't think I slept but I cannot be for sure. I got up the next morning thanking God that I made it through the night. I began to cook breakfast, some of Tyson's favorites, to try to ease the tension."

"Whew," I thought."

"That's when Tyson walked over to me and gave me a kiss on the cheek. Good morning, baby. How are you doing?"

"I'm great. Are you ready to eat breakfast?"

"No, I'm not that hungry. I'm just trying to sort out a few things."

"Like what," I asked. As soon as I asked, I knew that something was wrong. I should have just kept my mouth shut."

"I'm trying to figure out how you think that you could possibly leave me and make it on your own. You aren't the brightest."

"I turned around to look at Tyson just as he threw Patti's business card on the table.

"Last night, while you slept like a baby, I couldn't. I knew you were up to something so I did a little investigation of my own. What's the card all about, Kayla?"

"It's nothing really. I just went looking around at different places."

"Different places for what. Do you plan on moving?"

"Well, no, um, well maybe, I don't know."

"What's with all the gibberish? I asked you if you planned on moving."

"Um, I thought about it. I just priced some apartments to see what they were going for today."

"So did you plan of moving on your own or were we going together?"

"I wanted to move on my own." Kayla knew that by making the statement, it was opening up a can of worms. However, she couldn't help it. After last night, it was her only choice.

"So you think that you are going to be able to make it on your own, without me."

"I don't know but I am ready to try."

"What brought this all on, all of a sudden?"

"It's not all of a sudden. I have been thinking about this for a while. I think it's for the best."

"What do you mean that it's for the best? Who's best? What about me?"

"Tyson, you will be fine without me."

"Who says that I want to be without you?"

"It's obvious Tyson. All we do now is fight and I am tired. I need to leave this alone."

"You think that's possible."

"It can be if you let me go."

Tyson looked at me and didn't say a word.

"Tyson, I am always making you mad. We argue all the time and it's just not right."

"Aint' no relationship perfect. Everyone argues."

"That's not the point. I'm just tired, that's all."

"So what. You think that you are the one that can decide how this relationship is going to end."

"You decided it a long time ago."

"What do you mean?"

"Tyson, the first time you hit me, you decided it. You cannot possibly think that I would sit around here forever."

"You've been sitting here so far."

"That's because I didn't know better. I should have left a long time ago, the first time that you hit me. But I didn't."

"Why not?"

"Because I loved you but also because I didn't love me."

"So is that my fault, that's what you think. It's not my fault that you are a screw up. I have been trying to help you get a backbone for all of these years."

"That's my point. Why do you have to name call?"

"All I am doing is speaking the truth. Before I met you, you were screwing up. All your relationships failed. Your finances were all jacked up. You didn't know anything…"

Tyson was on a roll as he screamed insult after insult.

"See that's my point. You never have anything positive to say."

"I ain't lying, am I?"

Kayla had to look at her situation and yes, when she and Tyson met, she was in bad situation. However, it was now ten times worse.

"See, you cannot even argue back with me."

"Look, Tyson. I have had enough and I am leaving *today*." Kayla mustered up the strength to utter this word.

"Today?"

"That's right."

Tyson began walking over to Kayla.

"Today?"

"Yes, I am leaving." Kayla wanted to run out of the kitchen but could only walk slowly to the bedroom. She pulled out her suitcase and began filling it with the last of her essentials. Tyson stood in the doorway.

"So you are really going to do this?"

Kayla did not answer.

"Kayla. Kayla."

Kayla held her breath as Tyson walked closer.

"Baby, look, let's talk about this. I see that you are serious. You never packed your bags before. Turn around and look at me."

Kayla didn't want to look but she did. Tyson seemed to be sincere. His eyes were relaxed. Yet, there was an eerie feeling in the pit of her stomach.

"Sweetie, you need to go!" A faint voiced echoed in her mind.

"So you want to leave. OK, I'm cool with that. Let me help you pack." Tyson walked over to the dresser and began to pull the rest of Kayla's belongings out. "Here are your things." He threw them at her. Kayla tried to pick up the clothes but they were flying at her. She knew that she should just leave but these clothes were all that she had.

Tyson walked over to the closet and began pulling out her coats, sweaters, and pants. "I can't believe you have me helping you pack."

"You don't have to help. I'll do it."

"No, no. Let me." Tyson continued to fling clothing at Kayla and she continued to scramble for them. As he was flailing the clothes, Kayla was reaching down to clean up the mess. "Girl, get up. You have to get up now," The voice continued to speak just as Kayla looked up and saw that Tyson now held a belt in his hand. He reached back and came forward with a swoop. Kayla froze. She couldn't move.

"Kayla," Celeste interrupted "Are you saying to me that he tried to beat you with a belt?"

"Yes, that's what I am saying. I don't know what happened but as he was swinging, something stopped him."

"So what happened?"

He smiled at me. "You didn't think that I was going to hit you with this belt, did you?"

"I couldn't speak. All I could do was look. But something inside of me said to get up. Girl, I started running. I ran out of the house, without my suitcase. I didn't know where I was going but I had to leave."

"So what did he do?"

"As I was walking down the street, he followed me in the car. He kept saying Kayla, baby, I'm sorry. Can we at least talk about this?"

"I said nothing."

"Look, I lost my temper because I was frightened, baby. I don't know what I am going to do without you."

"I still said nothing. Girl, I was walking but didn't have a place to go. So I turned around. I figured if I turned around, then it would take him a much longer time to turn the car around."

"OK, look. Just listen to me. Hear me out and if you still want to leave, then I won't say anything. Just talk to me, please."

"As much as I knew that he was lying, I also wanted to hear what he was going to say. I don't know. There has always been a part of me that prayed that he would recognize what he was doing and feel sorry."

"So I stopped and listened to him and it was a bunch of crap. I stood by the passenger door because I knew that he would not be able to reach me."

"Tyson, I am still leaving."

"I moved away from the car and began to walk away. I don't know what possessed me to walk in front of the car, but I did to cross over to the other side of the street. That's when he hit me."

"He hit you."

"Yes he did. It wasn't a big hit but it was just enough to knock me down."

"A big hit?" Celeste retorted. "A big hit, a little hit. It's all the same. He hit you with a car. Do you understand that?"

"Yes, I do but he didn't drive into me."

Celeste looked at her friend in disbelief. She couldn't possibly minimize what happened. "You say it so matter of factly."

"I know." Kayla wondered why she seemed so detached from the situation. "I guess it's my way of coping with it all. It doesn't seem real to me either and I was there."

"Hmmph, I think about the first time that I met you." Celeste chimed in. "Do you remember?"

"Of course I do. I was attending group counseling sessions and you were one of our guest speakers."

"That's right. I didn't think that I would choke up like that but I could not help it. I gave my speech all the time but after listening to the women's stories, I realized that my opinions meant absolutely nothing. "

"Do you know on that day, it was the first time when many of us opened up and gave our testimony?' Kayla spoke. "We listened as you talked about your best friend Lisa and the guilt that you had for not stepping in. The only way that we could help you absolve that guilt was to give you the real reason why women stay. Celeste, there was nothing that you could have done to keep Lisa with you."

"How could you say that?" Celeste felt the tears burning her eyes.

"I can say that because we were all Lisa at one time or another. Do you remember Renee? She was the one with the glasses."

"Yes, I remember her. She said that her boyfriend put her out the house on the coldest night of the year… without any clothes. Now, you are probably wondering how such a thing could happen. It's simple. Remember when I spoke with you earlier about being uncovered. Every night when I lay down next to Tyson, I could never sleep with a gown. His reasoning was because he wanted to feel close to me. Now, I understand that it was so I could not get up and leave. Where was I going naked? It was also easy access to me when he decided to roll over, if you get what I mean,"

"Yes I do." Celeste felt her stomach crawl.

"But you see, that night, Renee needed to escape. She didn't care if she was as naked as a jaybird. She was so afraid for her life, that at that moment, she forgot where she was and how she was."

"I remember. Her husband had awakened her at three in the morning to accuse her of cheating, again."

"Not only did he accuse her, but he tried to choke her while she was asleep. Talk about sleeping with the enemy."

A chill ran down Celeste's spine.

"Then, there was Yazmin. Yazmin was the very pretty girl with long black hair."

"Oh yeah, I remember her. She was gorgeous but I could tell that she had no idea." Celeste replied as her memory was jogged.

"Exactly, mental cruelty is the worse of them all. Her boyfriend had beaten her down in more ways than one. "

"I remember. He would always accuse her of cheating."

"That's right. She went so far as to show us her scars. He would pinch her in her inner thighs. Can you imagine how painful that was? Even if she wanted to tell anyone, he knew that the only way she could prove it was to drop her pants. That night, Yazmin did just that."

Celeste couldn't hold back the tears. "How come? I remember watching Yazmin leave that night and knew that she was going back home. How could she go back considering everything?"

"It's hard to explain. Without speaking for anyone else, I know that there were times when I felt as if I was having an outer body experience. Yes, I felt the hits, the slaps, all of that. Yet, it didn't seem real. I died the first time he hurt me. When you love someone, you expect them to treat you with love and respect. Yet the first time they disrespect you, it changes who you are. You begin to question if they really love you or if it was all in your imagination."

"Now, I am a true advocate of the saying, *"if he hits you once, he will hit you again. And love is not supposed to hurt."* But it goes beyond this. When you are disrespected, but yet question the reality of it without action, it leaves you open to self-doubt. It opens the door to lowering your self-esteem. When they openly love you, you feel as if you can conquer the world. When they openly hurt you, you try to dig yourself down in a hole. "

"Sort of like an ostrich."

"Yeah, except the problem comes when you begin to question yourself and try to compensate. He has hurt you, whether it is cheating, name calling, or hitting, yet he is still around. You would expect that he would leave you if he doesn't love you. But no, this is the trick of the enemy. He will stay and might even apologize for his actions by saying that he lost control."

"Uh hm."

"So now you are doubting if you jumped the gun. The next time, you find yourself going a bit further to please him, in which ever way that he likes. Maybe you dress a certain way or you sex him a certain way. It doesn't matter because your boundaries begin to weaken. He'll hold off with the negativity for while but will test you in other ways. He'll think, "She stayed through that but will she stay through this." He'll be the best person that he could be until you become more relaxed. Then he'll test the situation one more time."

"You mean to tell me that this is a game."

"Of course it is. He'll create an argument to get you all emotional. He might call you names or attack you in some way. You will openly admit that you have only tried to love him and would bend over backwards to please him. Mind you, he already knows this. But you will need to verbalize it; this helps you convince yourself. He'll threaten to leave you because you are not worth it. You will work harder to please him so that he will stay. He will step up his game and do just a little bit more, you know, make it hurt just a little bit harder. You will do a little bit more, you know, work a little bit harder. It becomes a vicious cycle."

"So it is a game."

"That's right. You will do all that you can to make yourself worthy in his eyes. You will call him if you are late or just not go. You will change the way you dress so as not to bring attention to yourself. I have seen the prettiest girls dress in sack cloth so their men would not be jealous. You will compromise yourself just a little bit more."

"Now if you're a fast learner," Kayla continued, "then he will not need to hit you too often. Just enough to rile you up but not consistently. He will wait it out between episodes because you have acquiesced to everything he has suggested. To him you are the weakest there is and he has no respect for you. You feel that you are pleasing him, but you have not provided a challenge to him. Abuse is about control. He will create situations that cause you to second-guess yourself just so that he can justify his actions. All the while, you will feel as if you are going crazy because for the life of you, you don't see where you went wrong."

"So it's like he is punishing you for being good and loyal."

"Exactly," Kayla added. "He knows that he is wrong but he cannot control himself. If it is not you, it would be someone else or something else. He has abusive tendencies in many areas of his life. He could be a closet alcoholic or an open drunk. He can use drugs or surround himself in porn. Either way, there is some outlet for him that is deviant. He controls you because you are the easiest to tame."

"Wow. That's deep."

"I'm telling you. Don't get it twisted, abuse is color blind, you can be black, white, or green. You can be rich, poor, or in between. It doesn't matter."

"So tell me, why won't it stop? Even today, in 2007, it is as rampant as ever."

"It's simple. Women are afraid to tell their stories and seek help. Men are afraid to tell their stories and seek help. What you have to understand is that most abuse is hidden from the public eye. Judgment cannot come on the family because no one even knows that it is happening. There has to be an extreme case that makes everyone pay attention. Unfortunately, that is short lived."

"Why do you think things are like this?"

"I think it is because many people feel that it could never happen to them. They are invincible. Or it is because everyone has their own idea about boundaries. Some women will tolerate more from their mate if they are married to them. Nine times out of ten children are involved and the woman does not want to upset their world by separating from the spouse. Unfortunately, the best thing that a woman can do is to leave."

"You are so right. I remember that the worse domestic calls that I could receive are when there is a child involved. My heart would break each time that we had to remove the child to state custody. They only know that you are taking them from their parents, not the fact that their home situation is extreme volatile."

"It's sad, but children can adapt to the worst situations." Kayla interjected. "This is why I placed extra attention into their space here in the house. I tried to include all the things that help children stay young and innocent."

"You did a fascinating job of it."

"Why, thank you."

Just then, Minister Alexander and Sharee entered the living room.

"Kim and Jaynie, come here. I have someone that I would like for you to meet." Kayla began her introductions. "Celeste, our beautiful officer, has known me for several years now. She is a guest speaker for many domestic violence meetings that I attend."

"Hello, everyone." Celeste waved her hand.

"My best friend, Kim, and I have journeyed together for many years through our support group at the church. I chose this path while Kim, here, has chosen the path of ministry."

"Kayla, please," Kim interjected, "this right here is a ministry in itself."

"I was feeling the same way," Sharee agreed. "If anyone wants to know what heaven feels like, then they are pretty close to it right here."

"Why thanks you ladies, very much. It is greatly appreciated, especially coming from you both." Kayla replied.

Jaynie watched as these awesome women of God talked amongst themselves. Although they each served the public, they also served the Lord.

"Kayla," Jaynie interrupted. "Although I have not formally expressed my gratitude, I want to thank you so much for allowing me into your home. I really needed this."

"Jaynie, I already told you that *mi casa es tu casa*. You are truly welcomed. If you need anything, please ask."

"No, this is all that I need." Jaynie replied.

Kayla heard the surrender in Jaynie's voice.

"Jaynie, sweetheart, if I am not being too forward, please know that I truly mean that my home is your home. I cannot quite put my finger on it but the Holy Spirit wants me to tell you that specifically."

Jaynie immediately looked over at Minister Alexander. Had she shared her story with Kayla already? Did she know that Jaynie didn't have a place to go home to now that she had left James for good?

Minister Alexander looked over at Jaynie. "Jaynie, you know like I know that God moves in mysterious ways. All I did was bring you here."

"But, Kayla. How did you know?" Jaynie asked.

"I guess it's just a gift that God has given to me. In the beginning, I did not embrace it but now I realize that there is a look that we all carry; those who have been hurt beyond reason. It shows in our eyes."

Jaynie felt her eyes tearing, burning. A total stranger knew what was deep inside of her soul yet James did not have a clue.

"It's OK, sweetie. Let it out" Kim added on. Just like the sheep that know their Shepard's voice, we have to be able to see the women who need us. It's not about their words because we all know that silence reigns in our lives. It's all about the eyes and what they tell us."

Kayla interjected. "When fear creeps into our souls, it takes the brightness from out eyes, until eventually, there is no light at all. A hallowed expression seems to delve down into the souls of women who have been abused. Only the discerning eyes of those who have been there can see it."

"Am I that obvious? I thought that I had come out of it." Jaynie admitted. "I mean, I counsel the very women that you are talking about yet I cannot fix my own situation."

"That's the very problem that we need to overcome." Kayla interjected. "It is not about *us* fixing it. God is the only one that can fix it. We cannot even begin to understand just how deep the pain is for those that abuse others. Not just men, but women also. In fact, it is not for us to understand."

"Why do you say that?" Jaynie asked.

"I say that because if we knew the root of their pain, we will try to fix it. It's just our nature to do so."

"So what are we supposed to do? I mean, I love James, I still do. Even after the horrible names that he called me. I feel so bad about leaving him"

"Of course, you love him. He has already taken a place in your heart." Kim spoke. "However, where we fail is when we stop loving ourselves enough to get out of the situation. It's all about Love. When we stop loving ourselves, we also stop loving the one who has created us. God made each one of us in a special and unique way. He took the time to form each hair on our head. When we forget this, we forget the essence of who we truly are. When we allow ourselves to be abused, we have nullified our true essence. It is as if we do not matter."

"But I know that God told me to go home and to try to make it work." Jaynie rationalized.

"He may have told you to go home but it may not have been to make it work. We have to each face the very things that we once feared to see it for what it really is," Kayla spoke.

"Think about it this way, Jaynie." Kim continued. "God may have allowed you to go home so that you could finally move into the path that He has set for you. Prior to going back, you were well on your way onto being our counselor, and who knows, maybe a minister-in-training."

"Oh, please. I could never be a minister like you. I cannot even quote a scripture."

"You don't necessarily have to quote scripture to be a living example." Kim spoke. "Jaynie, I already knew that you were qualified long before you went home. However, you needed to see if for yourself. You understand the importance of forgiveness and could share your story with the world."

"I wasn't trying to be a martyr when I decided to go home. I was lonely and missed James. I wanted Lance to know his father. I wanted it to work."

"That's my point. All of your intentions were pure and good. You went home with the agenda of making it work. Unfortunately, James' intentions were not pure and they eventually surfaced. God needed you to see that. You were a new creature in Him and had a renewed mind to know that with God in the midst of your relationship, everything is possible."

"But it didn't work, did it?" Jaynie spoke sarcastically.

"No it didn't. But that's just fine because God can now use you as He should," Kayla spoke.

"How so?"

"Well, you are looking for a place to stay and my doors are open. You can help *minister* to the women who come through here. It has worked out perfectly because I know that they will truly be blessed to know you. I know that I am."

Jaynie looked from Kayla to Kim and back to Kayla again.

"Is this a trick?"

"Of course not." Both women spoke at the same time.

"I don't know." Jaynie had reservations. "You mean to tell me that I would be able to stay here with Lance, help the women, and speak about the goodness of the Lord."

"Hmmph. Girl, I wouldn't think about this too long," Sharee found herself chiming in. In all the time that had passed, she found herself mesmerized about the way that God had worked his stuff.

Celeste also found herself speaking up. "Kayla, I knew that you were awesome when I first met you. But to see how God has stepped in to bring you all together, I am just amazed. You go, girl." Celeste had to laugh as Lisa's anthem rolled off her lips. "This definitely calls for one of those sister-hugs."

Celeste, Sharee, Jaynie, Kayla, and Kim all shared a hug that not only embraced their souls but also intertwined their hearts. Their passion to uplift all women and bring them back to their rightful place with the Lord seemed to brighten all the dark crevices of their souls. This was definitely a part of God's plan.

"Uh, excuse me. I'm sorry for interrupting you all…" All the women turned around to face Jennifer. Dressed in a denim jumpsuit, she had curled her hair, taking special care to allow some hair to fall over her blackened eye. She used very little makeup to help hide the scars that were on her cheeks. She was a beauty to behold.

"Hey, Jennifer, sweetie." Kayla spoke. "I am so glad that you could join us. Lunch is just about to be served."

Jennifer watched each woman and couldn't help but feel the joy that was emanating from their beings. They seemed so at peace. How was that even possible?

"Thank you."

"As a matter of fact, ladies, let's head into the sunroom so that we can eat." Each woman followed Kayla into the sunroom. The glass walls gave a breathtaking view into a backyard that was blooming with flowers. A gazebo sat off to the side and held a covered gliding swing. The waters, filling the Olympic-sized pool with cascading waterfall, gently swayed in the breeze.

"Kayla, will you ever stop."

"Why, what do you mean?'

"I cannot believe that you actually have a pool."

"When I began to landscape the backyard, I did not plan on having a pool. But then, I thought about all the children who will be here. I knew that having a pool would be fun for them. Mind you, I could care less, since I couldn't swim. But the more that I began to see my dream manifest, I realized that if just for safety reasons, I would need to learn quickly. So I invested in classes and can now tread water. Although I am not the best swimmer, I do all right. If I need to save someone, I could."

"I never imagined that you would ever get into water." Kim spoke. "During one of our meetings, the ladies decided to share one thing that they were deathly afraid of and it couldn't be our significant others. I said that I was afraid of dogs and Kayla said that she was afraid of water. I remember asking her how this was possible if she showers and bathes everyday."

Kayla started to laugh. "Hmmph, I had to enlighten old girl. There are ways that you can shower without having the water run into your face. I always felt as if I was choking."

The women began to laugh.

"Then she went on to ask me how I could possibly be afraid of dogs," Kim spoke. "Let me tell you, Cujo can come in many sizes, especially, with those little chihauhuas. They are the meanest dogs that I have ever seen."

"That's true. I believe poodles come in at a close second," Jaynie agreed. "Hmm, let me see. What am I deathly afraid of? I guess I would have to say, heights. I get woozy while standing on a chair to get something out of the cabinet. I always think that I am going to fall."

"That's exactly why we had the discussion in class." Kayla spoke. "There are many things that make us feel uncomfortable and out of our element. We become so afraid if we even think that we have to encounter them. Whether it is drowning, being hurt, or falling, we do all that we can to protect ourselves. We avoid those situations at all costs. However, what we find out is that the same care that we use to avoid these situations, we throw to the wind when we stay in abusive relationships. We allow ourselves to feel choked, be hurt, and knocked down. Once we learn that fear comes in different packages, we can learn to conquer it. Learning how to swim did that for me. Although Tyson has been out of my life, I was able to conquer my fear of him by conquering my fear of the water. It wasn't easy. I have to admit that I wasn't the easiest student, however, I made the attempt."

"That's right," continued Kim. "Although I will never have a dog as a pet, I don't cringe as much when I see them. My niece has a cute Yorkie that I actually held the other day. Not for too long, mind you."

"Let me see," Jaynie added. "I still have to reach the top cabinets in my kitchen but now I use a step ladder, which is the proper tool to use. It's sort of like relying on God's word to help you through the times when you feel as if you are going crazy. Wow, I get it. My world has come crashing down all around me and I feel as if I am going to topple right along with it. Yet, if I stand on God's word, I will have the proper foundation. Hallelujah."

Sharee decided to jump into the conversation. "I guess that I am deathly afraid of being alone. Can you all offer me some advice?"

"You have answered it already." Celeste was amazed at how quickly she was able to offer a response. "Ladies, let me see if I can get this right. Sharee, you say that you are afraid of being alone, but you need to realize that you are never alone. God is always there waiting on you to call His name. He never imposes himself but waits patiently for you to seek Him first in all of your decisions. Once you realize that he is there, you will never feel alone."

"Yes siree. You nailed it on the head." Kayla screamed. "Who knows, there may be a spot for you at the Soul after all."

"Yeah, I could work security," Celeste laughed.

"You're already doing that by bringing women here. You are protecting their souls until they can finally come home to the Lord."

In an instant, Celeste remembered Lisa's last words. "It's time for me to go on home." She started crying. "You all may think that I am crazy, but my best friend Lisa told me that I helped bring her back home to the Lord. This was right before she died."

"And you did," Kim spoke. "You were the vessel that helped lead her back to the Lord. Your words healed her soul and protected her. You interceded on her behalf and she was saved that night, right before her death."

"I never looked at it that way." Celeste thought about it. "I guess that my biggest fear is losing the ones that I love."

"Have you ever thought of the idea that you are not losing them but are returning to their rightful owner, God himself?" Kim continued. "When you go on your calls, you meet so many women who are lost souls. When you share your life story with them, you not only are living Lisa's last dying wish, but you are also moving into your purpose, the purpose that God has set before you. Please don't ever think that it is your uniform. Your kindness and sincerity overshadows your uniform. Your pleas reach into a woman's soul.

Although not every woman heeds your warnings, there will be a few who will. Like Jennifer here."

Jennifer looked up from the table when she heard her name. Although she sat quietly at the table, she eavesdropped on their conversation as if she were a fly on the wall.

"Jennifer, sweetie. I hope that we are not making you uncomfortable." Kayla spoke.

"No, you are not. I am just taking it all in." Jennifer answered. "I guess that I can add that Officer... Celeste really touched me when shared her life story. She gave it to me plain and didn't pull any punches. I guess when she made me look into the mirror, I had no choice but to face my fear. My biggest fear is looking at myself in a mirror. It hurts too much."

"Jennifer, there are so many people who are afraid of their own reflection." Kayla spoke. "A mirror is powerful. It shows everything, from the black heads to the cellulite. Although it can show our imperfections, a mirror can also highlight our assets. Have you ever sat in the chair of your beautician as she spins you around to see her creativity? Voila. You gasp because she has made you look like a queen. You look good. Unfortunately, recreating her look can be very difficult but it doesn't seem to matter at that moment. You hold onto it as long as you can, sleeping on your elbows so your head won't touch the pillow."

All the women have to laugh at this because they have all been there.

Kayla continued "But what you will learn is that the more time that you spend looking in the mirror, you can create a new look for yourself that can become your own. It can be duplicated. You will see that you are fearfully and wonderfully made. God took the time to perfect you in His own image. And even in the times when you feel your worse and the crying doesn't seem to stop, Psalm 56:8 says that God still manages to bottle each and every tear. Your tears are precious to Him; each and every salty drop. Its salt helps to purify your soul and preserve your spirit until you are able to laugh again."

"And believe me, you will one day laugh again," Kim confirmed. "I look at my life and I thank God that my joy has come back. My love for my husband is even stronger than it was before because it is truly from my heart. A heart that had been broken for many years, not just by my husband, but because of my disconnection from its Source. God is the one that gave me a pulse again because he raised me from my succomb to death."

"Jennifer, sweetie, you too will come out of this situation a much stronger, confident woman. We are all living testimonies to that, although each of our situations are different. Just give us a chance to prove it to you," Kayla spoke.

"Prove it to me?" Jennifer spoke. "You have already proven to me. I look at each of you and actually feel hopeful. Although I am unsure of how it's going to be done, I cannot help but feel your excitement.

"And you should, sweetie." Kayla confirmed. "When you decided to come here with Celeste, you chose life instead of death. You chose to trust in the Lord and not rely on man. Although you question how it will be done, you have recognized that with God, all things are possible."

"That's right, Jennifer" Kim agreed. "Your faith is going to lead you to do such wonderful things, I promise you. And we all plan of having your back because we have all been there, in one way or another."

"I don't know what to say. I haven't felt this much love in a long time." Jennifer admitted.

"And to think, that this is only the beginning. God shall complete the work that He has started in you," Kayla spoke with assurance. "and Jaynie, those words are meant for you as well."

Jaynie felt her spirit quicken and knew that it was truth.

"Hallelujah, hallelujah."

The women began to praise the Lord for his grace and goodness. Hugging one another, they began to speak life into the ears that were listening.

April 17, 2006.

"Ladies and Gentlemen, we are truly blessed by this union, no let me change that, by this *reunion* between two of our most dedicated servers. Minister Alexander and Minister Roberts. Kim and Benjamin, it is now time."

Kim and Benjamin joined Reverend Holmes in the front of the sanctuary. Opting for a simple ceremony to exchange their vows, several family and friends came out to New Hope of Life Missionary Church to share in this wondrous event.

"Let us all give them thanks and praise for sharing their lives with us all. Although it had once been filled with fear and violence, our Lord has certainly given them a new song in their life. One that they have not been afraid to sing to the whole world. We thank you both for your transparency."

"Amen. Praise God. Hallelujah" echoed through out the sanctuary.

"Kim, please speak to your husband."

"Benjamin Roberts. Words cannot express how blessed I am to stand beside you on this special day. God has truly done a new thing in you and I am so proud to be your wife. You are my best friend for life and forever more. I stand beside you with confidence and faith that you will allow God to direct your path. I proudly sit under your covering knowing that you will protect me, love me, and keep me. I rest safely in your heart and in your arms and can dream once again."

"Benjamin" Reverend Holmes directed his attention his way.

Clearing his throat, Minister Roberts spoke. "My wife, Kimberly Alexander. I thank God that you chose me to love. You are such a precious gift from the Lord to me that sometimes I feel as if I need to pinch myself. I thank God that your faith has helped to mold me into the man that God has made me to be. Sometimes I feel unworthy of your grace and loving kindness because of who I once was. But I thank God that I am not the same. Your warmth has melted my heart. Your gentle spirit has soothed my spirit. Your passion for others, your passion for Christ, your passion for me has ignited my soul. I love you sweetie and I will live the rest of our lives to show you how much."

"The love that has been exchanged between these two is just the example that we all should remember about our Lord God" said Reverend Holmes. "He loves us all in spite of who we are. When we put our faith and trust in Him, He will cover us and give us rest. I tell you that God is awesome. There is none other like Him and there never shall be. His grace and loving kindness should give us a new confidence, a bolder walk, because we know that we are unworthy. Yet, He has redeemed us all and made us new. I tell ya, the Lord…" It was obvious that Reverend Holmes was on a roll and was ready to preach.

Kim and Benjamin didn't want too appear rude but this was definitely not the time for that. They were ready to become one once again. Reverend Holmes must have felt their heat.

"Excuse me all, I digressed for a moment." Everyone laughed because this was not the first time that he had done this and it definitely wasn't going to be the last.

"Now let's get back to it," said Reverend Holmes. "Without further delay, Kimberly Alexander, it is time that you return back to your former title, Kimberly Roberts, as I now pronounce you husband and wife. Benjamin, God has reestablished your privileges and she is now yours once again. You must always honor her and love her just as the Lord loves you. Seek Him first in all that you do and know that He will grant you all your wishes.

Applause rang out as the congregation cheered. The members of Women of Destiny and Brothers Helping Brothers because to praise God with a fervor that could not be reckoned with. This union also bridged the gap between both groups.

Reverend Holmes cleared his throat. "You all must know that we cannot forget some traditions." Turning to Minister Roberts, "Benjamin, you may now kiss your bride." Cheers now became catcalls and whistles.

"That's what I have been waiting to do all morning," said Benjamin.

"That's what I have been waiting for all morning," echoed Kim.

Jaynie, Celeste, Sharee, and Kayla couldn't do anything except smile as they watched Kim blush uncontrollably. Who would have thought that after all of these years, she would still melt at the thought of being in her husband's embrace. Jennifer sat quietly with a smirk on her face, a fierce haircut, and new wardrobe.

As this chapter closes, there are still so many unanswered questions. The Soul is the place where we can cast our burdens down and rest in the Lord. It is also the place where dreams are rekindled and lives are changed. It's inevitable, because when God is present, every knee shall bow and every tongue shall confess. So did Sharee close her heart to Robert? Does she understand that abuse comes in many different forms? Did Jaynie move into her ordained position of Counselor? How about Jennifer? As a newbie, it is so hard for her to slip back into a world that is dangerous, yet familiar. How I wish that I could fill you in but unfortunately, I cannot. God has not revealed it to me yet. Nevertheless, I move on through my own journey in life with expectancy, seeking revelation knowledge. This book has been in my spirit for many years, yet, I was afraid to release it into the atmosphere. Although it promised healing to my soul, I was not quite ready to receive it. Yet, the time has come when I can embrace my past and love me, inspite of me, just as the Lord loves me. Isn't that awesome? To be loved in spite of who you are. It is just as awesome to give love to others, in spite of who they are. So I thank each and every woman that I have met on my journey in this life. I thank each and every man that I have encountered on my journey in this life. Your presence has caused me to take one final glance at my past without God so that I can give my full attention to my future with God.

I dedicate this book to our Almighty God. He gets all the glory for it. I thank Him for ordering my footsteps and allowing me to come through experiences that can alter most without bitterness or regret. Originally written in 2006, I had no idea that I would be given another opportunity to share my life with others once again. After completing my book in 2006, I had no idea what my future would bring. I was just grateful that I was able to survive. Fast forward to 2024, my gratitude to my support system has not changed one bit. The only thing that has changed is that I am experiencing a loving, healthy relationship with my husband, Marty. Thank you for loving all of me and allowing me to laugh once more. You have been able to see the joy in life and I am blessed and honored to be your wife. I thank my family and friends for supporting me even though they did not understand the pain that I was going through. I thank my counselors from both the Domestic Violence Hotline and New Birth Missionary Baptist Church. Michelle, you taught me how to embrace my pain and Minister Munoz, you taught me how to forgive. Even though it has been 20 years, your counsel and wisdom is infinite. I cannot forget the ministry that I received during this time in my life. God has an appointed time for everything and we have finally reached it. Rebecca, thank you for being my second set of ears and eyes through this process of reintroducing myself to the world again without regret. Danette, you know I am so grateful that we can sit back and finally look at how our lives have shaped us into the strong women that we are. I love your resilience. Veronica, I remember the times when we were afraid to dream, but look at how God has given us so many opportunities to bring that sparkle back into our eyes. Keymia, we've shared our hopes, dreams, and vulnerabilities throughout the years and have watched how God continues to show Himself to us. Heidi, Machell, and Collet have each seen me during the best and worst times of healing and I could not have done it without you all. Linda, Jeanie and Jim, thank you for being there for me without judgment. There are those sister-friends who may have all gone on different paths, yet they remain forever. Robyn, Nagoya, Octavia, Celecia and Maria all still have a special place in my heart. Out of sight does not mean out of mind.

To my sisters and brothers (Valerie, Penny, Garry and Larry), we have grown closer to one another over the years and I appreciate all of your support. Val, thanks for allowing me to share my fears and laughter. Cammy, my Godsister, I love our weekly conversations about life, love, and God. Mo, we share so many good times. To my sons, William and Patrick, I am so proud of the men that you have become. This has been a journey for us all and my prayer is that you treat others with love and kindness. Last but not least, I give honor to my mother and father, Lawrence and Dorothy McCrear. Not having you here has been difficult, but I know that you are both cheering me on from Heaven. To the readers of this book, I thank you too. Abuse of any kind is not an easy topic to share with others, regardless of your position as the abuser or receiver. Every facet of your life will be affected, yet it is a subject that many tend to shy away from. Sharing my past, present, and future with you all has shown me that joy will definitely come in the morning, if we allow ourselves to embrace the process of pulling back the scars and allowing God's embrace to become the balm to our wounded souls. Although this is not the typical romance novel, it is the best one yet because being loved by God and being in love with God is the best place that you could ever be.